THE CLASSROOM TEACHER'S TROUBLE-SHOOTING HANDBOOK

Practical Solutions to Problems with Students, Adults and Procedures

JEROME C. YANOFF

To Marge
Good luck with your classes
Jerome C. Yanoff

arthur coyle press
chicago, illinois

The Classroom Teacher's Trouble-Shooting Handbook

Copyright 1999 by Jerome C. Yanoff

All rights reserved. No part of this book may be reproduced, distributed in any form or by any means, or stored in a database or retrieval system without written permission from the author or his representative. Reviewers who wish to quote brief passages in connection with a review for professional journals, magazines, newspapers, television or radio broadcasts may do so with proper credit given to the author and the Arthur Coyle Press.

Arthur Coyle Press
P.O. Box 59435
Chicago, IL 60659-0435

Edited by Mary Edsey.

Printed in the U.S.A.
First printing 1999.

10 9 8 7 6 5 4 3 2 1

Publisher's Cataloging in Publication Data

Yanoff, Jerome C.
The Classroom Teacher's Trouble-Shooting Handbook / Jerome C. Yanoff
  Includes 192 pages and index.
  ISBN 0-9665947-0-3

  1. Teachers.
  2. Teacher-Student Relationships.
  3. Classroom Management.
  4. Student Teaching.

371.1024   98-93687

Contents

Introduction iv
About the Author v
How to Use This Book vi
Additional Questions vii
I.   Problems with Students 1
II.   Problems with Special Education Students 77
III. Problems with Yourself 87
IV. Problems with Colleagues 109
V.   Problems with Administrators 121
VI. Problems with Parents 131
VII. Problems with Procedures 145
VIII. Problems with Unions 159
IX. Suicide 167
X.   Fighting 177
Index 183

Introduction

Beth Perry, a school nurse, was visibly upset:
> While I was teaching a health lesson to the special education students, several of them began swearing at each other and at me. The special education teacher did nothing to stop them.

Judy Long, a fourth grade teacher at a suburban elementary school, was disturbed by her principal's action:
> He is going to place a boy with cerebral palsy in my class. No one has been able to tell me much about the child or what I should expect of him.

Jack Johnson, a student teacher in a high school history class, was perplexed by a recent situation:
> When I reprimanded a girl for talking during my lecture, she just picked up her books and walked out. I tried to be assertive by telling her she had to sit down, but she ignored me.

Anne Green, a new math teacher, whispered a concern to a colleague:
> Mr. Smith made another pass at me this morning. I have already told him twice to stop. I don't know what to do about this. He's been a teacher here for a long time and is a close friend of the principal.

A teacher's day is filled with unexpected events. Children are always unpredictable. Colleagues and parents can be unpredictable as well. It seems obvious that teachers should expect surprises, yet when they occur many are unprepared.

Some teachers may show their confusion. Some may do something they later regret. Some may do nothing at all.

Though college courses may train teachers in lesson plans and educational psychology, the solutions to everyday classroom problems are often left to the teachers' resourcefulness with unpredictable results. Sometimes a teacher may seek advice from a more experienced colleague, but in many situations such help is unavailable. This book has been written to be a teacher's desktop experienced colleague—a colleague who is always available to help solve an immediate problem or offer advice on a problem to come.

The problems presented in this book are based on situations that actually happened to the author, his student teachers or his colleagues. The solutions are based on the accumulated experiences of the author and his fellow teachers during his 30 years in the profession.

About the Author

Author Jerome C. Yanoff taught in public school classrooms since 1966. He served for ten years as the union representative in his school, and six years on the executive board of the Chicago Teachers Union. He has been elected several times as a delegate to the Illinois Federation of Teachers and the American Federation of Teachers. He is currently teaching education courses at several Chicago area universities.

How to Use This Book

This book is divided into ten sections, each in a different area of the teaching experience. Some sections deal with students while others cover problems caused by school procedures, parents, or other adults in the school. Because of their importance, fighting and suicidal behavior are discussed in two special sections. Coping with these situations has unfortunately become a part of a teacher's job, and although difficult to discuss, cannot be ignored.

The introductory page to each section lists principles on which the section's problems are based. If teachers create their own solutions, they should base them on these principles.

Each problem is presented with the same format. Though the reader may be tempted to go directly to the solution, it is important to first understand the problem's source and analysis. The reader will then be able to adapt the given solution or a personal solution to a specific problem, solve it, and reduce the possibility that the problem will occur again. The format is as follows:

Problem: Presented in conversational form, each scenario covers a broad range so that it is applicable to diverse classroom situations.

Whose Problem: Understanding the source of the problem is essential to reaching a good solution. Many teachers feel they have the responsibility of solving every problem that arises in the classroom. The teacher is responsible to see that a resolution is reached, but sometimes that resolution should be reached by another person, perhaps with the teacher's guidance, perhaps not.

It should be noted that people who have problems often try to pass their problem on to someone else so they won't have to solve it themselves. Students may pass problems on to their teachers. If the teacher solves the problem for the student, there is a good chance the problem will reoccur, and she will have to solve the problem again. If the teacher is experienced enough to see this, she can give the problem back to the student and help him solve it.

For example, a student asks the teacher's help because he forgot his lunch money and is now hungry. The teacher has the choice of arranging to get some food for him or guiding him to find a way to get his own food. Unfortunately, many teachers would choose the first option, thus saving the student from being hungry. It might be better to help him discover what he must do to get some lunch. Though a more difficult task, it will reduce the likelihood that he will forget his lunch money again.

Analysis: The cause of the behavior should be a major factor in deciding how the problem is to be resolved. Each problem does not always have the same cause. Therefore, a number of possible explanations are presented to help the teacher find the most appropriate solution for the situation.

Do: Possible solutions which have proven successful are suggested. They are not the only solutions to the problems. A teacher may choose to use them as written or as a starting point to find other solutions to similar problems with varying circumstances. If a teacher feels she has a better solution than the one given, she should be willing to try it.

Do Not: These are responses which are inappropriate for the situation. They either punish the student, avoid the problem, or call for the teacher to act unprofessionally. Such responses are not helpful and might make the situation worse. Some may alleviate the problem in the short term but cause harm in the future. To avoid these responses, take a serious look at the likely consequences of using them.

Related Problems: Problem numbers and titles are listed for similar problems whose information may be helpful in determining solutions.

Additional Questions?

Please send a description of additional problems you would like to see addressed in subsequent editions of this text to:

>Jerome C. Yanoff
>c/o Arthur Coyle Press
>P. O. Box 59435
>Chicago, Illinois 60659-0435

Chapter I

Problems with Students

◆ *Each student is valued as an individual.*

◆ *The teacher is on the students' side.*

◆ *Each student must have the opportunity to develop a sense of responsibility.*

◆ *Students can develop self-esteem by successfully meeting challenges. The teacher's role is to provide the challenges.*

◆ *School is a place of learning. Students who exhibit inappropriate behavior demonstrate they have not yet learned to behave properly. The teacher's responsibility is to provide this instruction.*

Problems with Students

♦ 1 ♦
Aggression

Problem: I have a student in my class who is having family problems. Because of this he acts out in my class—arguing, swearing, threatening other students. I understand this is due to the pressure he feels, but I wonder how much longer I should let it go on. It is starting to bother some of the other students.

Whose Problem: The student's.

Analysis: One of the ways a person protects himself from emotional pain is to act aggressively. However, a child must learn that this is self-defeating behavior. The boy needs to realize that if he behaves in this way, his friends will abandon him—despite his need for their friendship at this time. He must learn to get along with others, even when he is under stress. The teacher may not be able to help him with his home situation, but can prevent him from making things worse in school.

Do: 1) Let the boy know that your classroom is a safe place for all, including him, and that he is not to threaten his classmates. 2) Tell him you understand that things at home are not going well for him at the moment, but that he has friends here who are on his side. Try to get him to separate his home situation from school. 3) If he is being hostile, you may have to set some limits for him and even define some consequences. This may give him some measure of security and a feeling that someone cares about him. 4) He may feel like talking about his situation. If he does, listen sympathetically and give him support. 5) If you are not comfortable in this role, recommend he talk with some other adult in the school, particularly a school counselor.

Do Not: 1) Do not allow the situation to continue. 2) Do not be more lenient with him than you are with the others. 3) Do not punish him. 4) Do not involve his parents.

Problems with Students

♦ 2 ♦
Apologizing

Problem: I have a student in my sixth grade class who is not a problem student. However, when he does something wrong he can't apologize.

Whose Problem: The student's.

Analysis: Some children are taught that to apologize is a sign of weakness, inadequacy, or inferiority to the person receiving the apology. Such children may fear the humiliation an apology might cause. This child may also be in conflict. If he thinks he has done something wrong, he may feel guilty and have a need to correct the situation by apologizing. It will be easier for the student if the problem can be worked out alone with the teacher.

Do: 1) Try to get him to apologize to the other person. Tell him he can practice on you. 2) If he can't do that, see if he will write "I'm sorry" on a piece of paper. 3) If he cannot do that, try to get him to explain to you what it is that is stopping him. Let him know that being able to apologize is a sign of maturity and strength. 4) Enact an apology and see if he will repeat the words. Ask him how it sounds when you say the words "I'm sorry" to him. 5) If this is not working it is best to drop it and tell him that you hope he can give an apology at a later time.

Do Not: 1) Do not force him to apologize. 2) Do not embarrass him in front of the class or another student.

♦ 3 ♦
Attention Getting

Problem: I have a student who acts out in my class quite often. I think he does this to get attention. It was suggested that if I ignore this behavior it will eventually go away. I have been trying this solution, but his behavior persists.

Whose Problem: The student's.

Analysis: Continual acting out may be a sign of a student's need for attention. Ignoring this behavior long enough will eventually make it go away, but may not be best for the student. He has a need for the teacher's attention. Ignoring him implies the teacher is not going to attend to this need. If this is the intention and the behavior is ignored, expect that initially his acting out will increase and then gradually decrease until it is gone.

However, it seems odd that when children are thirsty we give them water, when they are hungry we give them food, when they are dirty we give them soap and water, when they are tired we provide them with a bed for sleep, but when they need attention we ignore them. It is not bad, wrong or out of place to give a child extra attention. He only needs to learn to get attention in an appropriate way.

Do: 1) Recognize that this child needs attention and that you are capable of giving it. 2) Provide him with appropriate ways to gain attention. Make him a classroom helper. Give him a seat close to your desk so he can feel near to you. Pair him with another student who can satisfy some of these attention needs. There are many possible solutions that teach the child to ask for attention rather than to demand it. 3) If the child is mature enough, discuss his behavior with him so he can participate in improving it.

Do Not: 1) Do not allow the acting out to continue. 2) Do not try to extinguish his need for attention. 3) Do not feel that needing extra attention or giving extra attention is bad.

Problems with Students

♦ 4 ♦
Borrowing Money from the Teacher

Problem: One of my seventh grade students told me he forgot his lunch money and wanted to borrow two dollars from me.

Whose Problem: The student's.

Analysis: A student asking for a loan may make the teacher feel uncomfortable. There are feelings of concern for the student mixed with hesitancy about lending money. Consequently, the teacher could feel both discomfort and guilt, and ultimately submit to the stronger of the two.

Do: 1) Before lending a student money, answer these questions:
    a) Can I afford to lose this money?
    b) If this student fails to return the money, will my feelings about him change?
    c) Am I willing to ask him to return the money at a later time if he doesn't return it on his own?
    d) Am I willing to have other students ask to borrow money?
2) If you have answered no to any of the questions, tell him you prefer not to lend money to students. It is not necessary to explain or apologize. 3) If you have answered yes to all four questions, lend the money. Perhaps you could also give him a classroom job so he could earn the money. 4) Handle future requests on an individual basis. 5) Be aware of students who are frequently forgetting their money and asking for loans. If you are giving or lending money to students, you may be enabling them to continue coming to school without their own money. Denying the student's request may help him be more responsible in the future.

Do Not: 1) Do not tell the student that it is against school policy to lend money unless that is really the reason for your refusal. It is better to take full responsibility for your decision. 2) Do not tell the student you won't lend him money because you have been burned in the past by other students. This assumes he will not return the money and punishes him for what others have done. 3) Do not take on the responsibilities that the students should assume for themselves.

Problems with Students

◆ 5 ◆
Calling Teacher by First Name

Problem: I have a student in my room who calls me by my first name. I have corrected him several times, but he insists on doing it.

Whose Problem: The student's.

Analysis: This student is being intentionally provocative. His action is inappropriate. Either he is curious to see what will happen, or he is purposely being disrespectful. His payoff is that he gets a reaction from the teacher. This could be a power struggle in which case he must be confronted.

Do: 1) Inform him privately and very firmly that he will no longer take the liberty of addressing you by your first name. Do not allow him to question this. It is now a rule. 2) If he breaks this rule there will be a consequence. There is a strong chance that he will test this. He may tell you he slipped. Apply the consequence to help him remember. 3) If he persists, especially in front of others, you may have to challenge him publicly. Remind him that he had been warned and that you are sorry to see his conduct has not yet improved. Review with him that mutual respect is a class rule that will be followed. 4) If this problem still persists, consider notifying a school administrator and/or his parents.

Do Not: 1) Do not allow the situation to continue. 2) Do not get angry. 3) Do not insult the student. 4) Do not do anything in front of the rest of the class before you have exhausted every possible way of resolving the issue privately.

Related Problems: 43 Power Struggles, 138 Teachers Who Are Called by Their First Names.

◆ 6 ◆
Chasing a Student

Problem: One of my second graders has a hard time staying on task. She is in the habit of leaving her work table and running to the other end of the room. She then tries to get me to chase her to bring her back to her table. I have done this a couple of times, but she is very hard to catch. This is disruptive for the rest of the class, but I feel I have to do this.

Whose Problem: The student's.

Analysis: The girl's agenda may be to avoid doing her work. She does this by engaging the teacher in her child's play. As long as the teacher is chasing her, no work is being done and the situation is in the student's control. She may have a problem which is beyond her control and requires special attention.

Do: 1) Insist that she stay at her table unless she receives permission to leave. This puts you in control. 2) Emphasize that she is expected to do her work. This should be the focus, not struggling to get her back to her table. If the behavior persists, consider that she may have an attention deficit disorder or a behavior disorder. 3) Monitor her behavior and, if you feel it necessary, refer her for learning or behavior problems testing.

Do Not: 1) Do not chase her around the room. 2) Do not get angry at her. 3) Do not accept unfinished work from her.

Related Problems: 30 Impulsive Behavior.

♦ 7 ♦
Cheating

Problem: I caught a student cheating on a test.

Whose Problem: The student's.

Analysis: At least the teacher knows the student wants to pass the test. This is certainly better than not caring at all. The student has made a bad choice. He wanted to get a good grade but didn't attempt to do it honestly. He does not understand that school is about learning, not good grades. The grades should only reflect how much he has learned. He needs to be taught this.

Do: 1) Take the test away immediately. It is no longer valid. 2) Tell the student you want to speak to him when the other students are done. He can spend the remainder of the test time sitting quietly while everyone else is working. This will give him the opportunity to reflect on what he has done. 3) After the test, tell him you are disappointed in the way he acted. He can retake the test tomorrow, and he should study for it tonight. However, because he is getting a second chance, he will earn only 75% of his test score. This way he still takes the test but is penalized for cheating.

Do Not: 1) Do not cause a big scene. 2) Do not remove his chance to learn the material and retake the test. 3) Do not cross examine him or give him a sermon. 4) Do not tell him you are disappointed in him, only in what he did.

♦ 8 ♦
Chewing Gum

Problem: Several of my students chew gum during class. I was always taught that gum did not belong in school. It is difficult to keep the students from bringing it. I don't know if this policy is worth the effort.

Whose Problem: Perhaps the teacher's.

Analysis: Many schools have a rule against chewing gum. There are, however, some benefits to allowing it. It can relieve tension and reduce the desire for a cigarette in students who smoke. There are also many reasons for not allowing chewing gum in class. The sight of students chewing may be annoying to the teacher. It may interfere with the classroom process. There are good reasons to have rules about chewing gum. However, it should not be a rule just because the teacher learned it should be a rule.

Do: 1) Unless there is a school-wide rule about chewing gum, decide for yourself whether you will allow it. You may ban chewing during some activities but not during others. 2) Enforce that rule whether it is difficult or not.

Do Not: 1) Do not ban chewing gum because it was banned when you were a student. 2) Do not give up on enforcing rules because they are hard to enforce.

Related Problems: 132 Rules.

Problems with Students

♦ 9 ♦
Class Clown

Problem: A student in my class plays the role of the class clown.

Whose Problem: The student's.

Analysis: The class clown is very much like the class goat. Playing a role which isn't very positive is better than playing no role at all. The class clown may be a little more clever, a little more resourceful, and, consequently, a little easier to handle than the class goat. His role is a less dangerous and more acceptable. However, because there is so much positive reinforcement from the rest of the class for this role, it makes it difficult for the class clown to change his ways. There is not a lot a teacher can do. People don't change unless they want to change, and there is little reason for the clown to change.

Do: 1) Give the student some responsibilities and opportunities for leadership. This will give him the chance to try another role which he may find more rewarding. 2) Compliment the student for jobs well done, especially those accomplished in other roles.

Do Not: 1) Do not challenge him publicly about his position in the class. 2) Do not do anything that will reinforce the role of class clown.

Related Problems: 10 Class Goat.

Problems with Students

♦ 10 ♦
Class Goat

Problem: There is a boy in my room who is smaller than the other boys. They all pick on him. Sometimes they are very cruel.

Whose Problem: The boy's and the other students' in the class.

Analysis: It is no accident that everyone picks on this boy. Observation will show that he is setting up many of the incidents that are happening to him. Perhaps he tosses out an insult when things are quiet. Maybe he does things wrong when people are depending on him. These actions provoke others. He may not even be aware that he is doing this. The other boys begin to play their part. They help him to act this way, and then they jump on him when he does. Most of the time it is playful, but sometimes the situation gets out of hand and people become cruel. This is the role he has made for himself. He feels it is better to be a goat than to have no role at all. It is easier for him to keep this role than to try to develop a new one. The teacher won't be able to help him change until he decides he wants to change.

Do: 1) Approach the boy after someone has done something that hurt him. Tell him you have noticed that the others give him a hard time, and you would like to see it stop. Ask if he would like people to stop making fun of him. 2) If he is agreeable, work out a program with him. Explore together what he said or did that made the other person react so strongly. If he doesn't know, tell him what you have observed. Together you can make him more aware of how he gets the other boys' attention. By helping him control this behavior, you will be able to eliminate these experiences. 3) Provide support. When the student stops being provocative, it is likely that the other boys will provoke him. This is because they are accustomed to having him be the goat, and they are comfortable with it. Encourage the boy to work very hard to avoid setbacks when the others begin to provoke him. 4) Work out a signal that will remind him of his goal. 5) Remind anyone who is being insulting that this is not permitted. You expect your students to respect their classmates.

Problems with Students

Do Not: 1) Do not allow the present situation to continue. 2) Do not be too punitive with the students involved in this situation. 3) Do not discuss this situation in front of the other students. 5) Do not try to help the student if he doesn't want any help.

Related Problems: 9 Class Clown, 40 Passive Behavior, 62 Tattletale.

Problems with Students

♦ 11 ♦
Correcting the Teacher

Problem: I have a student in one of my classes who is always trying to catch my mistakes and correct me. I don't mind this happening once in a while. I am not insecure about making mistakes in front of the class. However, he corrects me so often, it has become annoying. And when he is wrong, he argues with me or hedges on his correction.

Whose Problem: The student's.

Analysis: Sometimes the teacher makes a mistake and the class catches it. This shows the teacher is human. It also gives the students an opportunity to test their independence—daring to correct the teacher. If the student who has made the correction is thanked, it will help build their self-esteem.

But a student waiting to pounce is a different matter. He has issues with power. He may also have problems with self-esteem; who is smarter, he or the teacher. This behavior is both disruptive and provocative. It cannot be allowed to go on.

Do: 1) Tell the student privately that correcting the teacher is not helpful. This behavior is inappropriate and must stop. It is disrespectful whether or not he means it to be. 2) If he says it is your problem because you can't stand to be corrected, tell him he is there to learn the lessons, which is not happening because of his disruptive behavior. 3) If he does not stop, inform your principal and/or his parents. He may repeat the charge that you are sensitive about your mistakes. Hold to your contention that you are concerned with his behavior because it is disrupting the entire class.

Do Not: 1) Do not embarrass him in front of the class. 2) Do not bargain with him. 3) Do not give him any power which you should have.

♦ 12 ♦
Crush on the Teacher

Problem: There is a girl in my eighth grade class who seems to have a crush on me—at least that's what I think from the way she has been behaving. This makes me a little nervous.

Whose Problem: No one's.

Analysis: Crushes are common, especially for children at the age of puberty. Usually teachers are unaware of their students' crushes, but sometimes the students' behavior is more overt or a little clumsy and easy to see.

Sexual attraction to another person is somewhat threatening to children at this age. Consequently they look for someone who is "safe." Very often it is a movie star or a pop singer who they can "love" without fear of being hurt or fear of having to act sexually. Developing a crush on a teacher is a little more daring but still safe. The students feel the teacher is so remote that nothing could happen to them as a result of their crush. It is a part of growing up. Fortunately a crush like this is usually short lived. The student will soon realize the teacher isn't interested in her. She'll feel terrible for a while and then discover someone new. What did she ever see in a teacher anyhow? Soon her love interest will be someone her own age.

Do: Nothing

Do Not: 1) Do not talk to the girl about her crush. 2) Do not do anything to encourage it.

Related Problems: 83 Crush on a Student.

Problems with Students

◆ 13 ◆
Cult Member

Problem: A student in my high school homeroom is involved with a religious cult. I don't think her parents are aware of this. I'm not even sure I should get involved.

Whose Problem: The student's and her parent's.

Analysis: It is easy to say that this is a family problem, and the teacher and the school need not be involved. However, if teachers are interested in the well-being of their students, they must involve themselves on some level.

This is something teachers should be concerned about, but not necessarily worried about. More needs to be known. A teacher should tread lightly because they are dealing with religious preference. Consequently, if there is no harm being done to the student, the teacher cannot intrude without her permission.

Do: 1) Show an interest in the girl's cult-related activities. If she would like to talk about them, inquire about the beliefs and practices of the group. 2) Ask if her parents are aware of her beliefs. If they are not, it is a danger signal. Cults will often demand that their young members not tell their parents. This could be a sign the cult is taking advantage of her. Ask why she has chosen not to tell them. 3) Encourage her to tell her parents, or ask her if she would like you to tell them. If she says she would like you to keep it to yourself, there is not much you can do. 4) If something illegal is involved, the school principal and the police should be notified. 5) Give support to the family if they encounter difficulties with their daughter and her involvement with the cult. Help them gather information about the group she has joined. Your school counselor should have some information about new religious organizations and cults. You may also write to:

> The American Family Foundation
> P.O. Box 2265
> Bonita Springs, Florida 33959

Problems with Students

Do Not: 1) Do not ignore the situation. 2) Do not get into an argument with the girl. This will only cause her to entrench in her beliefs. 3) Do not feel she is doing something wrong because she believes in a religion which is much different than yours.

◆ 14 ◆
Depression

Problem: I have a student who is very depressed. She sits in her seat and stares at her desk. She seems out of touch with the rest of the class. I really feel sorry for her, but I don't know what I should do.

Whose Problem: The student's.

Analysis: Depression can be temporary due to a recent incident. If there is some problem which has just happened in the student's life, such as a death or divorce in her family, then it is natural for her to be depressed. In fact, depression is an essential part of her recovery, and a lack of depression would be a source of concern. At this time the student is unable to function well in school. She is focused on a current problem and must reach a resolution in her own way.

Depression can also be a chronic condition with many possible causes. It may be caused by a chemical imbalance, which can be helped with medication. There may be a psychiatric problem, which needs exploration and possibly treatment. The teacher's concern is that this girl is not learning in her classes, and this should not be permitted to go on indefinitely.

Do: 1) Be available with a sympathetic ear. If you are not comfortable doing this you can refer the girl to the school counselor. If this is a temporary situation following a disaster in her life allow her some time to get through her depression. Tell her that you understand that this is a difficult time and that you are there if she needs you. 2) Continue to give her class work. Tell her to do as much as she can, but not to feel under pressure to finish it. Let the girl know you are there to help her. Allow her to sit quietly at her desk or in another part of the room if she likes. 3) If this depression continues beyond two or three weeks you may have to help her stay focused on the material by sitting with her for a while. Be gentle. Praise the work that is done. 4) Notify the counselor about the situation. You and the counselor should also notify the parents about your concerns.

Problems with Students

Do Not: 1) Do not allow the situation to continue for more than two or three weeks. 2) Do not put pressure on the student to produce work. 3) Do not fail to notify school administration and parents if the situation continues.

Related Problems: 70 Depressed.

◆ 15 ◆
Divorce

Problem: One of my fifth grade students told me her parents are getting a divorce. She is very upset about this.

Whose Problem: The student's.

Analysis: Although divorce has become common, it has not become any easier for the children involved, particularly those of elementary school age. In addition to the disruption in the student's life, there are unanswered questions which shake her sense of security: which parent is going to move out? how often will she be able to see this parent? what is life going to be like for her now? She may wonder if she is going to have to choose one parent over the other. She may also wonder deep down if the divorce is somehow her fault. In addition, there may be fighting between the parents which affects her. She is under a great deal of pressure. The fact that the girl told the teacher about the divorce shows that she trusts the teacher. The teacher is an important person to her right now.

Do: 1) Be prepared with a sympathetic ear if she wants to talk to you once or twice. 2) If she doesn't approach you, ask her an open question such as, how are things? 3) If she has stopped talking to you or if she seems in need of a lot of your time, consider taking her to the school counselor. 4) Notify her parents if she exhibits any unusual changes in her behavior such as listlessness, depression or dangerous behavior.

Do Not: 1) Do not think the problem isn't serious. 2) Do not try to give her therapy on an ongoing basis. 3) Do not discuss the situation with her in front of other students.

Related Problems: 14 Depression.

Problems with Students

♦ 16 ♦
Drug Lecture

Problem: I was giving a lecture to my seventh grade class about problems caused by taking drugs. One of my students asked me if I had ever used drugs. I was so caught off guard that I didn't know how to answer.

Whose Problem: The teacher's.

Analysis: The student's question has nothing to do with the lecture the teacher is giving. The lesson is about problems caused by drugs—not the teacher's personal history.

In addition, the question is manipulative. If the teacher answered no, the student would ask, "How do you know drugs are bad if you never tried them?" If the teacher answered yes, he would ask, "What right do you have to tell us never to use drugs when you have used them yourself?" Some students may also have difficulty reconciling the knowledge that their teacher used drugs. Answering this question looks like a lose-lose situation with neither answer being much better than the other.

Do: 1) Ignore the question because it is personal and does not necessitate an answer. 2) Stay focused on the topic of the dangers of taking drugs. This is a health problem. You are concerned with their health. They need to have clear minds for your classes.

Do Not: 1) Do not answer an inappropriate question by telling stories about your personal experiences. 2) Do not become moralistic about drugs. 3) Do not get sidetracked from the subject. 4) Do not feel that every question requires an answer. 5) Do not tell your students you have taken drugs. You become living proof that a person can experiment with drugs and turn out all right.

Problems with Students

♦ 17 ♦
Dying

Problem: I have a student in my class who has cancer and a year to live. It is painful to have her in my class. What is the point of continuing her education? What am I supposed to do with her?

Whose Problem: The teacher's.

Analysis: This is a very difficult situation which can push a teacher to the limits of professionalism. A dying child makes everyone very sad and even afraid. At times a teacher may try to create distance from the child to avoid the pain and discomfort. It would be easier to bear this death if the teacher were not close to the child or involved in her life. It would be so much easier if the teacher didn't have to see her almost every day, and worry about her on the days she didn't come to school. Some teachers would become closer to the student and others would distance themselves from her. The latter would ask questions such as, "What is the use of educating this child?"

Do: 1) Make this student's last days as pleasant as you can. For most children this means coming to school, being with the other children and acting like everyone else. The class should make the dying student feel she is wanted and part of the class. It is a good idea to speak with the student and her family to see what they would like. As the teacher, you play an important part—not only for what you can give the dying child, but for what you can offer the other children as a role model. They will all be looking at the teacher to see how she handles this experience. 2) Be prepared to answer the other students' questions about death and be ready to listen to any feelings they want to express. It is important that someone they trust is there for them all the time. 3) Inform your students' parents of the girl's condition so they can give support to their children. 4) Confide in the class that at some time the girl will leave, never to return. It will be very sad for everyone. Ask the family what they feel is the best way to handle final good-byes. 5) After the student is gone, you should discuss with the class how they feel and how you feel. The class may want to go to the funeral. They may want to organize a memorial event. They

Problems with Students

may wish to raise money to purchase something for the school in the girl's name. 6) Keep your school counselor and/or administrator aware of the emotional state of your class.

Do Not: 1) Do not let your personal feelings stop you from giving professional service to the dying student and the rest of the class. 2) Do not neglect to give support to the dying child and the rest of the class. 3) Do not neglect to provide some closure for the class after the student dies. 4) Do not neglect your own emotional needs.

♦ 18 ♦
Epilepsy

Problem: A boy who experiences epileptic seizures is being transferred into my class. I understand these seizures can get pretty violent.

Whose Problem: The school's.

Analysis: The only problem here is that no one has told the teacher what to expect or what to do. Epilepsy is not rare, so it is a good idea to have some knowledge about it. Children who have epileptic attacks should inform the teacher, so the teacher can be prepared to help.

Do: 1) Discuss the facts and myths of epilepsy with your school nurse. Learn about gran mal and petit mal seizures. Inquire about the type of seizures this student has, the medication he takes, the likelihood of an occurrence in the classroom and the procedure you should follow. You will probably be asked to notify the nurse or administration so they can take appropriate steps. 2) Meet with the parents and discuss, along with the child, what they would like you to do and what you feel you can do. You may be required to do nothing more than make sure he doesn't bump into anything. Ask the parents if you may inform the rest of the class that an epileptic seizure might happen. 3) If the boy's epilepsy is controlled by medication, have him promise to tell you if he hasn't taken it. Children on medication often experiment by skipping a dose to see if they will be all right. 4) If the child's parents have consented, discuss epileptic seizures with your class. Watching an epileptic seizure can be very frightening to a child who doesn't understand what is happening. 5) Assure the other students that the situation is under control. 6) Prepare members of the class to help if a seizure does occur by moving furniture out of the way and notifying appropriate people in the building.

Do Not: 1) Do not be afraid of the situation. 2) Do not make the student feel you don't want him. 3) Do not make the student feel he has to handle a seizure by himself. 4) Do not forget there are other children in the class who may become upset if they witness a seizure.

♦ 19 ♦
Father's Day Presents

Problem: I wanted my class to make little gifts for Father's Day. My principal suggested that we shouldn't do this because so many of our students do not have contact with their fathers. She felt this might set up two classes of students, those with fathers and those without. I feel we should have something for the fathers, especially since we made Mother's Day presents just a couple of weeks ago.

Whose Problem: The principal's.

Analysis: There are probably numerous circumstances existing between your students and their fathers. Some students may have fathers or surrogate fathers but may not wish to present them with a gift or card. Some may have strong bonds with their fathers or surrogate fathers and may want to give them a gift or card. Some may not have relationships with their fathers but may have resolved this in their own minds. Some fathers may feel hurt or excluded if they don't get a gift or card from their child, especially if the mother received something on Mother's Day.

Do: Prior to Father's Day allow the students to create gifts or cards to present to anyone they wish.

Do Not: Do not think you must avoid a project because it may hurt your students' feelings. Students who are accustomed to not having a father will handle this very well on their own. Consequently, your fears are unfounded. Those students who are new to this situation will learn to cope with it. Having them avoid the situation will not help them.

Related Problems: 15 Divorce.

Problems with Students

◆ 20 ◆
Foreign Student

Problem: Our class is getting a new student from Africa. He speaks little English and knows little of our country's customs.

Whose Problem: The student's.

Analysis: This is a wonderful opportunity to teach your new student about the ways of this country and the rest of your students about another culture.

Do: 1) Welcome your new student. 2) Assign a different class member each day to show him how things are done. 3) Encourage all students to help him learn English. 4) Let the new student tell the class about his culture. 5) Invite his parents to visit and discuss their country. 6) If time permits, do projects related to his country and culture. 7) Ask him to teach the class some of his language while he is learning English.

Do Not: 1) Do not feel you have to acculturate this student all by yourself. 2) Do not make the student feel uncomfortable about his differences. 3) Do not make the new student fend for himself.

Problems with Students

♦ 21 ♦
Gangs

Problem: A student in my seventh grade class is talking about joining a street gang. I'm not sure if he wants to join, is being pressured to join, or is just trying to sound like a big shot.

Whose Problem: The student's.

Analysis: Unless a person has been part of the gang culture or has grown up near it, the full extent of a gang's attraction and power is difficult to fathom. Its pull is very strong, especially among children 11 to 16 years old who need to identify with a group.

Gangs give their members a sense of identity, protection, social affiliation, purpose, and even reason for being. They are a source of power and money. In schools with a large gang presence, they are part of the students' culture. To the child who does not have aspirations or has given them up, the gang provides a sanctuary as well as an opportunity for personal and financial success.

For children who have dreams of entering the American mainstream, the gang may be an obstacle to their goals. Children who don't want to join a gang but are pressured into joining may be in danger of bodily harm or death if they refuse. Sadly, these are the same threats which they face if they do join the gang.

Do: 1) Try to stop the boy from joining, even if it seems futile. Inform him privately that it is wrong to be in a gang, and you are opposed to his joining. He already knows the reasons for not joining better than you know them. Express your fears to let him know that someone cares about him. 2) Discuss this with his parents. Some parents would rather move the entire family to a new home than allow a child to join a gang. Help the parents formulate an action plan. 3) Report the boy's comments to your administrator to see if there are any other options available, such as social workers who may be able to work with the boy. 4) Always be aware of students who want to become gang members. The earlier you begin talking to them, the better chance they will have of staying out. 5) Have a discussion about gangs with your entire class and let them know your feelings about joining one.

Do Not: 1) Do not ignore the situation. 2) Do not feel totally powerless. 3) Do not give a lecture to the boy about gangs.

Problems with Students

♦ 22 ♦
Ghetto English (Ebonics)

Problem: I have a student who speaks only Ghetto English. I can understand him, but I don't know if this is good for him.

Whose Problem: The student's.

Analysis: Use of Ghetto English in the classroom has been controversial. The prevailing opinion is that Ghetto English should be considered a legitimate language. If Standard American English is a variation of the King's English, so is Ghetto English. It is an integral part of a culture whose people take pride in their speech. Capital letters are even used in reference to it.

However, a student who doesn't speak Standard American English will have trouble coping in this society. College entrance examinations are given in Standard American English. Many businesses are not willing to hire individuals who cannot speak Standard American English. It appears likely that a teacher could be handicapping a child by allowing him to use only Ghetto English and not Standard American English.

Do: 1) Allow the student to continue using Ghetto English, but insist that he know Standard American English as well. 2) Make sure he learns the language skills he needs to attend college or get a job. 3) If there are many students in your school who speak only Ghetto English, meet with the rest of your faculty and devise a plan to improve the students' use of Standard American English.

Do Not: 1) Do not think that speaking only Ghetto English is all right. 2) Do not feel that learning Standard American English is too difficult for your students. 3) Do not shame or ridicule the students for the way they speak. 4) Do not infer that Ghetto English is a non-legitimate or inferior language.

Problems with Students

♦ 23 ♦
Gifted

Problem: I have a very bright girl in my class. Regular class work and additional enrichment work do not challenge her. Double-promotion is not a solution because the next grade's work won't challenge her either. Besides, she is one of the smallest students in my room, so placing her with older students may not be a good idea. Our school does not have a gifted program.

Whose Problem: The school's.

Analysis: One of the principles of our education system is that students with learning problems need to receive help to perform at grade level. This means that our schools not only help slow learners so they move up to grade level, but they also neglect bright students so they don't get too far ahead of grade level.

Our country has over four million students classified as "special needs students." They are eligible for special funding, special programs, and special teachers to help them reach their full potential. Gifted students make up less than 5% of this group. The federal government has mandated funds to provide assistance for all students with special needs with one exception—the gifted are ineligible. Our country is often critical of the European and Asian school systems because they ignore their weakest students. We, however, are guilty of ignoring our strongest.

Gifted students sometimes present another, more subtle problem. Their abilities may intimidate teachers who fear they cannot meet the students' needs. Consequently, the teachers may deny the abilities of their gifted students, so they won't have to teach them at the appropriate level.

Do: 1) Work with the parents' group and faculty to develop a program for the gifted students. This begins with a decision to identify and nurture these students. Keep in mind that "gifted" not only means smart, it also means talented. 2) Allow gifted students to depart from regular classroom curriculum. Modify their homework and seatwork involving drill. Consider waiving some parts of their curriculum. 3) Encourage them to develop their own projects in school and in the community, especially in real life situations. 4) Permit gifted students to move among classrooms to take advantage of their strengths. A gifted fourth grader could

Problems with Students

take his math class with a higher grade. 5) Make it possible for them to do group work with their classmates, so they can develop leadership and organizational abilities. 6) Instruct parents about their role in providing enrichment for their children. 7) Encourage the district to develop a gifted program.

Do Not: 1) Do not give gifted students additional busywork. 2) Do not insist on making a gifted student adhere to the standards of the rest of the class. 3) Do not make a gifted student the "teacher's helper." 4) Do not be intimidated by the gifted student's abilities.

Related Problems: 117 Considers Child Gifted.

♦ 24 ♦
Hatred towards the Teacher

Problem: There is a student in my class who hates me. She glares at me and makes insulting remarks to her friends. She speaks loud enough so I can hear her comments, but never says them to my face. I don't know what I have done to cause this.

Whose Problem: The student's.

Analysis: There is a good chance that the girl's actions have little or nothing to do with the teacher, especially if the teacher has no idea what is causing her behavior. The teacher might remind her of someone she doesn't like, such as a parent or other family member. The teacher may have unknowingly hurt her feelings—perhaps said or did something inadvertently that she considered terrible. Whatever the cause, her actions are inappropriate and interfere with her success in class. The more she shuts the teacher out, the more instruction she is missing.

Do: 1) Tell her you have noticed she is keeping her distance from you and that you are sorry because you need to work with her. If she can tell you what is troubling her, you can both try to resolve it. If she is uncomfortable she may want to get away from you, but at least you have begun to break down some of the barriers. There is a good chance she will start to accept you if you are open and available to her. 2) If she doesn't accept you, seek help from your school counselor or another adult. In spite of your efforts, she may act this way for the rest of the year. Unfortunately, this may be unavoidable.

Do Not: 1) Do not automatically feel it is your fault. 2) Do not try to make things up to her. 3) Do not feel you must resolve the problem. 4) Do not be insulting or mean to her.

♦ 25 ♦
Hitting Another Student

Problem: I saw one of the boys in my class reach out and hit another boy. It wasn't a fight, just one good punch. It wasn't playful either. The boy who got hit was obviously in pain.

Whose Problem: The hitter's.

Analysis: Hitting is inappropriate. The hitter's behavior can be explained in several ways: an incorrect response to frustration, a challenge to classroom order, or a physical reaction to what cannot be expressed verbally. However, the reason for the hitting is not the issue. The concern is that the hitting stops.

Do: 1) Call the hitter to you immediately. Ask him three direct questions: what did you do? what should you have done? what will you do next time? Make it clear that hitting is not allowed. 2) If the hitting was unprovoked, then an apology is necessary. If, however, the hitting was provoked by another student, then both students are equally responsible, and an apology may not be necessary. 3) Give a consequence and instruct the child to return to his seat.

Do Not: 1) Do not ignore the problem. 2) Do not try to get to the bottom of the problem. 3) Do not delay taking action. 4) Do not allow the dispute to continue. 5) Do not seek additional information from other students.

Related Problems: 2 Apologizing.

Problems with Students

♦ 26 ♦
Hitting That is Culturally Accepted

Problem: In my homeroom there are two teenage students who are going steady. They both come from the same European country where it is acceptable for the men to hit the women. I have seen the boy hit the girl on more than one occasion. Even though they both accept this practice, it makes me feel uncomfortable.

Whose Problem: The two students'.

Analysis: While hitting may be acceptable in their culture, this school is part of the American culture, and the teacher must preserve and instruct that culture. In this capacity, the teacher cannot permit the hitting to continue. There are many practices from other cultures that are not accepted and may even be against the law in this country. Suppose theft was acceptable to them. Should the teacher permit stealing in the classroom?

Do: 1) Tell them in the strongest terms that they will not be able to act this way in school. You do understand this is a part of their culture, but you and the school have rules against it. 2) Encourage them to do something besides hit when they become upset. There is a good chance that at least one of them will be very happy that you have taken the effort to intervene.

Do Not: 1) Do not allow the situation to continue. 2) Do not feel you should not judge a practice from a foreign culture. 3) Do not involve either the parents or the principal.

Problems with Students

♦ 27 ♦
Hitting the Teacher

Problem: I have a student who got so angry she lashed out blindly. I got hit. I don't think she did it on purpose.

Whose Problem: The student's.

Analysis: Hitting a teacher under any circumstance is unacceptable. When the teacher gets hit, the entire class watches to see the consequences. The students must get a very clear message that it is never acceptable to hit a teacher. If the teacher fails to act in this situation, it will tell the class that the teacher is not an important person. This could be threatening to the students who need firm limits and have behavior problems when they feel the teacher is not in control.

The reason for hitting the teacher must also be addressed: how did this girl get so angry? did the teacher have a part in this? was the girl trying to get out of a situation and couldn't? was there a power struggle?

Do: 1) Impose appropriate consequences on the student. 2) Let the rest of the class know that there was a consequence. 3) Notify the principal and the girl's parents. 4) File an assault report. 5) If it seems appropriate, notify the building union representative of the incident and its resolution.

Do Not: 1) Do not pass off the incident as being accidental or unimportant. 2) Do not hit back. 3) Do not blame yourself for having caused the incident. 4) Do not impose inappropriate consequences, either too harsh or too lenient.

Related Problems: 25 Hitting Another Student.

Problems with Students

◆ 28 ◆
Homeless

Problem: One of my high school juniors told me after class today that his parents had thrown him out of his home and that he needs some help finding a place to stay.

Whose Problem: The student's and his family's.

Analysis: The student needs help. He has expressed this by approaching the teacher with his problem. There is little the teacher can do for him personally. However, the school counselor or administrator should have the resources to help him connect with an agency that can help him. His family is still legally responsible for him. Throwing him out is not a legal option.

Do: 1) Take the student to the school counselor or an administrator. 2) Wait with him until he is connected with the proper people. It will demonstrate your support.

Do Not: 1) Do not tell the student it isn't your job to get involved in his personal problems. 2) Do not offer the student money to help him survive on his own. 3) Do not offer to take him home with you. 4) Do not try to mediate the dispute between your student and his family.

Problems with Students

♦ 29 ♦
Homework

Problem: Every time I assign homework to my high school classes, the students all laugh at me and tell me that I am wasting my time. They say they have no intention of ever doing homework and that I am lucky they come to school at all. I am starting to feel foolish for going on with this charade.

Whose Problem: The students'.

Analysis: The students are mistaken to think the teacher is lucky if they show up. Many people think that schools and teachers are solely responsible for the success of the students. A more reasonable view is that schools and teachers provide every opportunity for students to have a successful school experience, but actual success is the individual responsibility of each student.

It is the teacher's responsibility to provide the opportunity to do the homework. If the students decide not to do their homework, it is their decision. They are responsible to themselves and their parents.

Do: 1) Review with the class the responsibilities of a student. 2) Assure them that they have the choice of whether or not to do the homework, but that the homework is part of their grade. You would like to see them succeed. If they want good grades and if they expect to pass the class, they will have to do the homework. 3) Tell them they also have the choice of whether or not they will come to school. You hope they decide to come. If they wish to abandon school, they should make that decision with their families and know the possible results. Those who are staying will have to meet the expectations of the class.

Do Not: 1) Do not feel lucky that your students are showing up for your class. 2) Do not stop assigning homework because you don't expect it to get done. 3) Do not give your students anything less than a full measure of education. Do not "dumb down." 4) Do not feel the teacher is solely responsible for the success of the students.

Related Problems: 42 Poor School Work, 93 Successful Teaching.

Problems with Students

♦ 30 ♦
Impulsive Behavior

Problem: I have a student who always raises his hand when I ask the class a question. Most of the time he doesn't know the answer. Sometimes he has his hand up before I even finish asking the question. Then he laughs.

Whose Problem: The student's.

Analysis: As frustrating as it is, there is a good possibility that this behavior is not in his control. Impulsive acts such as these, as well as inability to focus attention and organize work, are common in children who have learning disabilities or attention deficit hyperactivity disorder.

It is also possible his behavior is a way of getting attention or gaining some control over the class. Perhaps he knows the teacher likes people who volunteer with the answer, and he wants the teacher to like him. He just doesn't make the connection between knowing the answer and raising his hand. He may also be purposely trying to annoy the teacher, or he could just be playing and meaning no harm.

Do: 1) If this student has reoccurring problems with impulse control, inability to focus and lack of organization, have him screened for both attention deficit disorders and learning disabilities. 2) If hand raising is the only problem you have with him and you find it annoying, it could be a power control problem. He is doing it to get you angry. Insist he stop the inappropriate behavior. Use either rewards or punishments to reinforce your action.

Do Not: 1) Do not get angry. 2) Do not embarrass the student in front of the class. 3) Do not take it personally.

Related Problems: 43 Power Struggles.

◆ 31 ◆
Insulting Another Student

Problem: Two of the children in my class are often very insulting to each other. Sometimes it is hard to tell if they are serious or just kidding around.

Whose Problem: The students'.

Analysis: Most of the time, students who insult each other are just playing. There is the danger that this play can lead to real anger and aggression. Insulting play is usually accepted behavior among children. However, if the classroom is a place where work is done in an atmosphere of respect, there is no room for this type of behavior.

Do: 1) Insist that insults, even in play, not be used in your room. 2) If your students are insulting each other in anger, calm them and let them cool down in silence. Tell them no one is to get the last word. Their insults are creating a bad situation where everyone will end up a loser. 3) No consequences or further actions are required.

Do Not: 1) Do not allow the situation to continue. 2) Do not try to get to the bottom of the dispute during class time.

Related Problems: 148-150 Fighting.

Problems with Students

◆ 32 ◆
Insulting the Teacher

Problem: One of my students called me a vile name and then swore at me.

Whose Problem: The student's.

Analysis: Though the teacher may have set off the student's anger, the student is acting inappropriately. While it is necessary to show the student that swearing at the teacher cannot be tolerated, the teacher must also examine her own part in the incident in order to decrease the possibility of this happening again. Was the student pushed too far? Was he losing face in front of his peers? Was he giving signals that he was under stress?

The rest of class will be waiting to find out the consequences of this incident. There must be a consequence or the class will get the message that it is all right to swear at the teacher.

Do: 1) Have the student come up to your desk immediately. Tell him you are concerned that he would talk to an adult this way and hope it won't happen again. 2) Ask if he can express his frustration in appropriate words. Help him with this. 3) When he is calm, ask for an apology. He may or may not be able to do this. Help him. 4) Ask him what he thinks is an appropriate consequence for what he has said. If he cannot think of one, give him an assignment or task. When it is finished tell him you are glad that he is behaving better, and you hope this won't happen again. 5) Try to resolve issues like this quickly. If you cannot, ask to speak with the offending student after school.

Do Not: 1) Do not pretend you didn't hear the swearing and name calling. 2) Do not swear back. Some teachers think that swearing back at students shocks them into giving respect. On the contrary, if the teacher swears it tells the students that it is all right to swear in class and at the teacher. 3) Do not take the insult personally or feel hurt. The insult is part of the student's outburst and is relevant to the student, not the teacher. 4) Do not punish the student too severely. 5) Do not involve the principal or parents unless necessary.

Related Problems: 2 Apologizing, 27 Hitting the Teacher.

Problems with Students

♦ 33 ♦
Juvenile Delinquent

Problem: I am getting a boy in my class who has a history of trouble with the law. I am a little nervous about this.

Whose Problem: The student's.

Analysis: This student has a reputation that makes people wary of him. Many teachers would also assume he would potentially cause problems. However, students like this can be productive members of the class. Their problems most often are caused by unresolved anger or the way they learned to act in their environment.

Do: 1) Assume this student is not going to be a problem. 2) Treat him as you would any other student. 3) Welcome him into the class. Introduce him to the students and acquaint him with the procedures and rules. Your class functions on a basis of mutual respect. You must respect him and expect him to respect you and his classmates. 4) Get him started on his work right away. Show him from the beginning that you expect work from him, and that your class has structure and goals you expect him to follow. 5) Let him see that people are succeeding, and that there are consequences following both good and bad behavior. 6) Be prepared if he should test the structure. Deal with him the way you would with any other misbehaving student. Have no hesitation about giving him a consequence. Tell him you expect better from him. 7) If breaking rules and showing lack of respect for others are becoming frequent occurrences, work harder with him. He can still be taught to behave. Tell him his behavior is having a negative effect on the rest of the class. He must take some responsibility. It may mean losing privileges, which he will have to earn back. It may be necessary to have a class meeting where the other students can confront him about his behavior. 8) If his poor behavior continues, recommend him for counseling or special education services.

Do Not: 1) Do not distrust the student without having a specific reason. 2) Do not ignore his bad behavior. 3) Do not give up easily. 4) Do not allow him to think his bad behavior doesn't matter. 5) Do not let him think that this school experience will be like all his previous school experiences.

Problems with Students

♦ 34 ♦
Lack of Attention

Problem: When the students take turns around the room answering questions, I find many are not paying attention.

Whose Problem: The students' and the teacher's.

Analysis: If the teacher goes around the room asking each student to take a turn, everyone will figure out which question they will have to answer. If the students are not interested in learning, their question will be the only one they try to answer. Students must have some interest in the material and a reason for learning it.

Educators spend millions of dollars trying to develop material that the students will find interesting and relevant. This is only dealing with the problem externally. The problem must also be dealt with internally. The students must find a way to learn the material because they see that learning is in their best interest.

Do: 1) Involve all the students in all the work. Try putting them into groups and making the entire group responsible for all the answers. Each group member should work to ensure that all the others are doing their part. The students will not only learn the answers, they will also learn to accept and distribute responsibility. 2) Communicate to the students that it is to their benefit to learn the material and develop a responsibility for doing the work. 3) Focus your teaching more on responsibility and less on finding correct responses. This gives the students the opportunity to learn about both success and failure. It is all right for them to experience failure if they can learn something from it. You can help them to avoid failure if you teach them not to accept it easily.

Do Not: 1) Do not feel that their success is totally your responsibility. 2) Do not be afraid to let them fail once in awhile.

Related Problems: 37 Motivating.

Problems with Students

♦ 35 ♦
Leaving Class

Problem: I was in the middle of teaching my high school history class when I had to reprimand a student for talking. She got angry and said she was leaving. I told her to sit down, but she walked out anyway. I feel as though I lost face in front of the whole class. They all laughed when she slammed the door behind her. I don't know if I can face this student or the class again without feeling embarrassed.

Whose problem: The student's.

Analysis: This type of problem is a good example of a power struggle—one person wins and the other loses. It is the teacher's job to instruct students about proper behavior, but the teacher cannot force the students to behave properly. A teacher who tries to force her students to behave the way she wants will experience many power struggles. Power struggles can and should be avoided.

In this situation the teacher gave good instruction when she told the student to sit down. The student couldn't follow the teacher's instruction. The teacher should not be embarrassed because a student couldn't behave. If the teacher instructs the students in proper behavior and responsibility, the students should learn to become responsible for behaving correctly.

Do: 1) Report the girl to the school office. 2) Have her parents accompany her when she is readmitted to your class. 3) Review the class' behavior with the rest of the students. 4) Give consequences to both the student who walked out and the students that laughed. They all must learn that their behavior was unacceptable. 5) In the future help students who get into power struggles. Once this student challenged you, she couldn't back down because she would lose face. You can prevent a student from feeling challenged. Tell the student that you hope she is not leaving the room—in other words, you are not going to stop her. Let her know that if she leaves you must report it, and you don't want to do that. If she does leave, tell the class you are sorry she could not do the right thing. Report the incident to the office.

Problems with Students

Do Not: 1) Do not let her go without reporting it. 2) Do not get angry at the student for not obeying you. 3) Do not allow the students to think it is all right to laugh at a situation such as this. 4) Do not feel you have lost face.

Related Problems: 43 Power Struggles.

Problems with Students

♦ 36 ♦
Lying

Problem: I have a student who lies to me so often that it has become impossible for me to know when she is telling the truth.

Whose Problem: The student's.

Analysis: This student has found it preferable to lie rather than tell the truth. The reason is not important. She must learn that a working relationship is built on honesty.

Do: 1) Explain to your student how difficult it is to communicate when you don't know whether she is being truthful. 2) Start assuming that she is not telling the truth. When she tells you something important, tell her you don't believe her. This will be very frustrating to her when she is telling the truth. 3) After doing this a few times, ask if she would like people to believe her. If she would, set up a program together to count the number of times she has told the truth. 4) Compliment her every time she does tell the truth. Tell her you hope that the next time she will also be telling the truth. Expect some lapses but persist.

Do Not: 1) Do not allow the situation to continue. 2) Do not become angry and frustrated. 3) Do not begin to dislike her because she lies.

Problems with Students

♦ 37 ♦
Motivating

Problem: My class is often unmotivated. Sometimes I can get them interested by involving them in fun projects related to the lessons. Most of the time, however, it is like pulling teeth to get them to do their work. I am running out of ideas.

Whose Problem: The teacher's.

Analysis: It is part of the teacher's job to motivate the students. This can be achieved with external influences such as activities that make learning more fun and enjoyable. However, the teacher must also influence the students internally by teaching them to motivate themselves.

Do: 1) Provide fun and interesting work. 2) More importantly, help the students understand that learning is good for them. Teach them to set learning goals. Help them see that they are attaining these goals and that this will lead to a better life for them. By learning these attitudes, the students become part of the motivation process.

Do Not: 1) Do not feel that the teacher is the only one responsible for motivating the students. 2) Do not allow the students to feel that their school work has no relationship to the rest of their lives.

◆ 38 ◆
Obscene Computer Message

Problem: We have a computer class for our junior high school students. One of the skills they learn is to communicate with other members of the class. One boy used this opportunity to send an obscene message to a girl on the other side of the room.

Whose Problem: The boy's.

Analysis: Though some adults may send obscene messages over the internet in the privacy of their homes, this does not justify obscenity in the school, nor should the school be a part of developing this behavior. Because this is an educational setting, students should be taught the social responsibilities of communication as well as the skills.

Do: 1) Bring the boy and girl together. Have the girl relate how she felt about receiving his message. 2) Let the boy know that an apology is in order, because obscenity on the computer is the same as obscenity spoken in class. 3) Ask him if he understands the correct etiquette for communicating with computers. If he doesn't, he needs to learn it. 4) If this is a single incident, consider the matter closed. If this behavior persists, stronger methods, such as involving the boy's parents or the school administration, may be required.

Do Not: 1) Do not ignore the matter because "everyone does it." 2) Do not involve parents or administration if it is an isolated incident.

Problems with Students

◆ 39 ◆
Off-Task

Problem: During my history lesson I noticed one of my students reading a novel hidden inside her textbook. Though I was happy to see that she reads novels, I felt she should be doing the lesson with everyone else.

Whose Problem: The student's.

Analysis: It is rewarding to see students reading for recreation, but they must learn that recreational time is earned. When a lesson is being presented, the student should be participating.

Do: 1) Compliment her on her choice of reading. If you are familiar with her book, you may ask if she would like to discuss it with you later. You might also recommend or offer other books she might enjoy. 2) Ask her to put the book away and do the lesson with the rest of the class. 3) If possible, work out a plan so that she can have recreational reading time in school when she finishes her lesson.

Do Not: 1) Do not let her continue reading the novel because you feel it is good for her to read. 2) Do not reprimand her for reading during class. 3) Do not confiscate her book. 4) Do not pretend you didn't see her reading.

Related Problems: 46 Recreational Reading in School.

Problems with Students

♦ 40 ♦
Passive Behavior

Problem: I have a student in my class who is very passive. It bothers me to see the other kids take advantage of him.

Whose Problem: The student's, the teacher's, or no one's.

Analysis: The student's passive behavior could have been learned at home. His family or their culture may value passive behavior. His behavior could also show the way he has learned to survive or be accepted in his environment, and this is the best he can do.

Do: 1) Establish whether you or the boy is having a problem with his passive behavior. 2) In either case, discuss the boy's behavior with his parents. It is their responsibility to decide the way they want their child to behave. Support their decision. Working against them will confuse the boy. 3) If the family decides their son needs to be more assertive, help him by providing opportunities where he can make his presence known in class. He might be put in charge of passing out materials or evaluating some classroom activity. 4) If it is your problem, examine why the boy's behavior makes you uncomfortable and try to resolve your feelings.

Do Not: 1) Do not decide on your own that the child needs to be more assertive and then push him towards it. 2) Do not belittle the child in hope of changing his behavior. 3) Do not act contrary to the wishes of the child or his parents.

Related Problems: 10 Class Goat.

Problems with Students

♦ 41 ♦
Physical Abuse

Problem: One of my students told me that his stepfather beats him. He has the bruises to prove it.

Whose Problem: The student's and his family's.

Analysis: In most states the law requires teachers to report suspected cases of child abuse. The fact that the boy has approached his teacher means he needs help and trusts the teacher. If he is let down, he may not approach another adult for help, at least not for some time.

Do: 1) Find out the procedure in your school for suspected child abuse. 2) Immediately report the student's statements to the school administrator or counselor. They will contact the proper authorities. You may be required to file a report or to give testimony. 3) Be prepared to give emotional support to the child for the next few weeks. There may be some repercussion directed towards the child when the family is notified of the charge. Support him by assuring him he has done the right thing.

Do Not: 1) Do not minimize the problem by telling the child not to worry. 2) Do not fail to notify school administration. 3) Do not attempt to handle the situation by yourself. The state has trained professionals to do this work. 4) Do not worry about giving testimony to the authorities. It is usually confidential.

Related Problems: 50 Sexual Abuse, 57 Suspected Abuse.

Problems with Students

◆ 42 ◆
Poor School Work

Problem: My entire class did poor school work this semester. I feel partly responsible, because I think I could have done a better job with them. I am thinking of raising all the grades.

Whose Problem: The students' or the teacher's.

Analysis: Teachers often mistakenly feel that they are solely responsible for the success of their students. Teachers must present the material effectively and set the structure for learning. It is the student's responsibility to learn the material.

Grades are meant to reflect how well the students achieved this. The teacher merely records these grades. If she inflates them, she insults her students by implying she doesn't expect very much of them. She rewards their mediocrity and teaches them that they will pass whether they work or not. This may give some students a false sense of how well they can do.

If the teacher has not done a good job of presenting the learning material, if it was uninteresting or below the standards for the age of the students, then the teacher needs to replan the classroom expectations and lessons.

Do: 1) Give the students the grades they have earned. 2) If they are angry when they receive them, it is a good time to devise a plan together for improving their work. Set goals and discuss how they can be achieved. 3) If you get complaints from the principal and some of the parents about the grades, be professional. Leave the grades unchanged. Tell the principal that you are all working on better results for next time.

Do Not: 1) Do not inflate the grades. 2) Do not feel that good grades are the sole responsibility of the teacher. 3) Do not feel that there is something wrong with your teaching if the grades aren't good. 4) Do not neglect to review and evaluate your work in the classroom.

Related Problems: 29 Homework, 93 Successful Teaching.

Problems with Students

♦ 43 ♦
Power Struggles

Problem: One of my students often engages me in power struggles. Today I asked him to pick up a piece of paper, and he refused. We got in a deadlock and nothing was accomplished.

Whose Problem: The teacher's and the student's.

Analysis: The bad thing about power struggles is that there is always a loser. Sometimes everyone loses. A teacher can easily win a power struggle, but in so doing may lose the respect of the student who has been forced to back down. The best that can be done in a power struggle is to break even.

Do: 1) Refuse to engage in power struggles. 2) Accept that you cannot force your students to do what you wish. You should instead ask for their cooperation. If a student refuses to pick up a piece of paper, pick it up yourself and tell him, "I'm sorry you couldn't do this." By doing so you will have shown your students that it is all right to pick up a piece of paper, and no one will be a loser. 3) If, however, a student threatens the safety of the class, you will have to assert yourself and demand the student back down. The security of the class is more important than avoiding a power struggle.

Do Not: 1) Do not get into a power struggle unless you absolutely must. 2) Do not get into a situation where you are arguing back and forth with a student. 3) Do not feel you have to control all the behavior in your class.

Problems with Students

♦ 44 ♦
Pregnancy

Problem: One of my students is pregnant. Is there anything special I should be doing for her?

Whose Problem: The student's, the teacher's, or no one's.

Analysis: Teachers may have personal feelings about students who are pregnant. It is sometimes difficult to hide those feelings. The mother-to-be may be unmarried; some teachers may feel this is immoral. Some may feel the pregnancy is the girl's fault, and she is getting what she deserves. Others may think she is in need of help and will want to offer advice and counseling. And some may think a pregnant student, married or unmarried doesn't belong in school at all.

Do: 1) Put your personal feelings aside. 2) Continue to work with her as would any other student. As a professional teacher you must educate all your students. 3) If she needs emotional support, give it to her, even if you cannot support the choices she has made.

Do Not: 1) Do not make the student feel uncomfortable about her pregnancy. 2) Do not give advice unless you are directly asked. 3) Do not give advice which is contrary to decisions reached by the girl and her family.

Related Problems: 48 Secret Pregnancy.

Problems with Students

♦ 45 ♦
Provocative Clothing

Problem: There is a girl in my sophomore English class who always wears very tight, revealing clothes. I do not feel it is appropriate for school.

Whose Problem: The girl's.

Analysis: People express how they feel about themselves in the way they dress. A student who wears provocative clothes shows a need to attract attention. Though her choices may be inappropriate, the federal courts have ruled that freedom to choose one's attire is covered under the First Amendment as a part of freedom of speech.

Do: 1) Tell the girl you feel that her attire is not appropriate for school. Offer suggestions on how she might dress. 2) If you have a good relationship with her, tell her you would appreciate it if she were to dress more appropriately. 3) If you feel she is mature enough, the two of you can discuss how others might view the way she dresses.

Do Not: 1) Do not pass moral judgement on the girl. 2) Do not insult the girl or make innuendos about her. 3) Do not threaten her if she refuses to change. 4) Do not involve administration. 5) If she refuses to change her style of dress, do not pursue it.

Problems with Students

♦ 46 ♦
Recreational Reading in School

Problem: My sixth graders don't enjoy reading.

Whose Problem: The students'.

Analysis: Rather than concluding that your students don't enjoy reading, it is better to assume that they haven't yet learned to enjoy it. In today's world, reading for pleasure is not always cultivated. Television and video games seem to be more popular attractions. Books are not read or even present in some homes.

A classroom teacher may feel that reading of any material should be encouraged. This is not entirely true. Reading should not be an end in itself. Children do not need a school program to interest them in reading comic books or popular magazines. They do, however, need a program that sparks their interest in quality literature. Unfortunately, some of these programs make reading competitive by rewarding the person or team that reads the most books. This competition encourages finishing books, not enjoying them.

Do: 1) Set aside a regular time to read books to the children. Let then get in comfortable positions. Start with stories which can be read in one sitting and gradually progress to longer works that require several days to complete. Take turns letting the students choose some of the stories. Some may even want to take a turn reading to the class. After each story, ask for volunteers to discuss what has been read. Show enthusiasm. If the teacher is enthusiastic, the students will be too. 2) Visit the library during one of the reading periods. Have the librarian show the students around, then allow time for the students to find books for themselves. 3) If possible, establish a weekly reading period where everyone, including the custodial and lunch-room staffs, stops all work to read a book they have brought with them.

Do Not: 1) Do not feel the situation is hopeless. 2) Do not develop a program where reading is considered a chore rather than a pleasure. 3) Do not assign book reports for every book students read. 4) Do not develop competitive reading programs.

Related Problems: 39 Off-Task.

Problems with Students

♦ 47 ♦
Running Out of Supplies

Problem: There is a girl in my class who seldom has school supplies. When I begin a lesson I see her trying to borrow paper or a pencil. I know her family can afford supplies. She just forgets to re-stock them. When she does bring supplies to school, she pays everyone back. She is also very generous when others need to borrow.

Whose Problem: The student's.

Analysis: A student who consistently borrows supplies is playing a control game with the teacher. She is trying to slow down the learning process by being disruptive. The child is well aware that she is running low on paper. She even gives it away so she will run out sooner. If the teacher shows frustration, the child has succeeded in winning the game.

Do: 1) Tell the girl you would like to help her get her supply problems under control. 2) Inform her that starting tomorrow she will no longer be allowed to borrow supplies in class. 3) Together set up a chart to record the supplies she has everyday. 4) She may run out of supplies at a crucial moment to test you. If so, tell her she will have to sit silently during class and do the work at home. If she cannot do the work at home, she will not get credit for the assignment. 5) This situation may make her angry. It would be wise to inform the principal and the girl's parents of this plan. 6) Continue to chart her supplies daily, even if the girl seems to have made progress.

Do Not: 1) Do not allow the situation to continue. 2) Do not give her your supplies. 3) Do not get angry or feel frustrated over what she is doing. 4) Do not punish her.

Problems with Students

♦ 48 ♦
Secret Pregnancy

Problem: One of my students told me she is pregnant. She doesn't want to tell her parents and doesn't want me to tell them.

Whose Problem: The student's.

Analysis: A young girl who experiences an unplanned pregnancy often doesn't know what to do. By confiding in her teacher the girl demonstrates that she needs and trusts her teacher and cannot handle this problem alone. However, parents are responsible for the welfare of their children. Working with the girl in secrecy could anger her parents enough to protest strongly to the school administrator or even make them take legal action. The teacher could become more personally involved than is appropriate for a teacher/pupil relationship. During an emotional crisis, any advice given could easily be misunderstood.

Do: 1) Encourage the girl to tell her parents. 2) Recommend that the girl go with you to the school counselor for additional help. 3) Support her in class by being more flexible in your academic demands than you ordinarily would be.

Do Not: 1) Do not reject the girl's initial request for help. 2) Do not try to handle her problem yourself. 3) Do not give a moral or religious lecture. 4) Do not become involved if the parents are not informed. 5) Do not condemn or dislike the girl for her behavior. 6) Do not push the girl into making decisions.

Related Problems: 44 Pregnancy.

Problems with Students

♦ 49 ♦
Selling Drugs in School

Problem: I am fairly certain that one of my students is selling drugs out of his locker.

Whose Problem: The student's and the school's.

Analysis: A student who sells drugs in school is breaking the law, misusing the school building, endangering the safety of other students, and disrupting learning. The boy and the other students must understand the boy's actions are wrong and drugs in the school will not be tolerated. Students who know of the boy's activities will be waiting to see how the adults will deal with him.

Do: 1) Notify your principal and the police immediately. They will search the student's locker according to proper procedure. The student will most likely be sent home pending his hearing. He should be suspended for a period of time and then allowed back under supervision. He may attempt to return to school the next day. Your school should have a policy preventing this. 2) Discuss with the other students what has happened to the boy. Allow them to express their feelings about students selling drugs in the school. Explain why you feel it is a bad idea. Remind the students that it is against the law and discuss the consequences the boy will likely face. 3) Make certain that your school establishes a policy for handling such problems if they don't already have one.

Do Not: 1) Do not allow the situation to continue. 2) Do not fail to notify the school administrator of your concerns. 3) Do not allow other students to think that it is all right to sell drugs in school.

Problems with Students

♦ 50 ♦
Sexual Abuse

Problem: One of my students told me she is being sexually abused at home by her step-father.

Whose Problem: The student's and her family's.

Analysis: There are two possibilities. If the girl is telling the truth, she is in a very abusive situation and needs immediate help. The fact that she has been able to approach the teacher with this is heroic in its own way. However, if the student is not telling the truth the teacher may unwittingly become part of a terrible family situation in which an innocent person is unfairly accused. His reputation is shattered, and he is left with little defense. In either case, the student has a serious personal problem. It is not up to the teacher to determine if the student is telling the truth or not.

Do: 1) Contact your administrator or school counselor at once. They will pass the information on to the proper authorities. 2) During the investigation provide moral support for the student. 3) When you are interviewed, it is important to report only what you actually know.

Do Not: 1) Do not decide for yourself if the accused person is innocent or guilty. 2) Do not dismiss or make light of the problem. 3) Do not fail to report the accusation to the school administration. 4) Do not attempt to handle the situation yourself. You do not have the resources to do this. 5) Do not discuss the incident with colleagues. 6) Do not entertain any feelings that you should or should not be getting involved. Remember, most states mandate that you report all forms of child abuse and this is certainly one.

Related Problems: 41 Physical Abuse, 57 Suspected Abuse.

Problems with Students

♦ 51 ♦
Slow Learner

Problem: A boy in my class needs a lot of help with his classwork. He is trying so hard. I want to help him, but I only have so much time to give.

Whose Problem: The student's.

Analysis: It is good that this student wants to learn. He should be accommodated. However, the method used shouldn't take the teacher away from the rest of the class for large amounts of time.

Do: 1) Give the boy extra attention but in a different way. Instead of staying with him until he has learned each concept, concentrate on getting help from other sources. Arrange to have his parents do extra work with him at home, or ask some older students to tutor him or act as an aid during class. 2) Have your students work in groups of three or four so they help each other.

Do Not: 1) Do not neglect the rest of your class to provide for one student. 2) Do not feel you are the only person who can teach your students. 3) Do not let the boy slip because you didn't provide the help he needs.

Related Problems: 76 Retarded.

Problems with Students

♦ 52 ♦
Smells of Marijuana

Problem: There is a student in my class who comes back from lunch almost every day smelling of what I think is marijuana.

Whose Problem: The student's.

Analysis: Marijuana is an illegal substance, so there is the potential risk of her being arrested. If the she is getting high during lunch, she is not receiving full benefit from her afternoon classes. If she is able to get high almost every day, other students may think they can do the same.

There is a chance she is not smoking marijuana but is with people who are. Your goal is not to find out whether she is getting high, but rather to see that she is able to function in class.

Do: 1) Tell her she smells of marijuana when she returns from lunch. It is not necessary to accuse her of using it. She would probably deny it and you don't need a confession. Let her know that you would be concerned if any of your students were getting high. You want all of them to be at their best when they are with you. 2) Tell her you are going to walk by her after lunch tomorrow to see if that smell is there, and you will continue to do so from time to time. She may become defiant and tell you that this is none of your business. Tell her that during school her activities, her health, and her state of mind are very much your business. She may agree or say nothing. 3) If she continues to smell of marijuana, tell her you are going to report this. Then follow through.

Do Not: 1) Do not allow the situation to continue. 2) Do not directly accuse her of smoking marijuana without knowing for certain. You will open yourself to legal problems and have to deal with a student who is accusing you of falsely accusing her. 3) Do not accuse her of being with people who smoke marijuana unless you know for certain. 4) Do not involve the principal, parents or police without giving her a chance to clean up her act on her own.

Related Problems: 54 Smoking.

Problems with Students

♦ 53 ♦
Smelly Student

The Problem: I have a student in my class who smells because he doesn't bathe. Some of the other students have noticed this and asked to be seated away from him. I am embarrassed to approach him about his lack of hygiene.

Whose Problem: The student's.

Analysis: There are two possibilities. One is that he does not know he smells. In this case he should be thankful you told him, even if it is embarrassing. The other possibility is that he is aware that he smells and wants it that way to keep others at a distance. This is a defense some people have. Either way, you should insist that he clean up.

Do: 1) Speak to the boy. Tell him people must bathe for good hygiene and good manners. Ask if there is any reason why he cannot bathe. Perhaps his plumbing is broken, his home does not have good bathing facilities, or his parents don't allow him to bathe very often. If one of these is true, notify his parents of the problem and request they find a way to have him bathe more often. If none of these reasons are true, demand that tomorrow he be clean, with clean hair and clean clothes. Tell him you are going to be aware of his hygiene every day. 2) Follow through. Compliment him quietly when he is clean. 3) There is a chance he won't come to school the next day. If so, call his parents and tell them what happened. 4) If he comes to school dirty again, have another talk with him so he knows you are serious. Tell him if he comes dirty the next day, you will contact his parents.

Do Not: 1) Do not allow the situation to continue. 2) Do not give a talk on cleanliness to the entire class for his benefit. Everyone, including the boy, will know who you are talking about. 3) Do not compliment him for cleanliness in front of the class.

Related Problems: 10 Class Goat.

♦ 54 ♦
Smoking

Problem: I think one of my sixth graders is smoking. I can smell cigarette smoke on her when she returns from lunch.

Whose Problem: The student's.

Analysis: A 12-year-old, sixth grader should not be smoking. It is bad for her health and against the law. She must be stopped.

Do: 1) Tell the girl that she smells of cigarettes. She can either admit or deny she is smoking. Tell her that whether she or her friends are smoking, you don't want to smell it on her anymore. Let her know that you are concerned because cigarettes are bad for her health. Add that you are going to be checking up on her. 2) The following day have her come up to your desk so you can see if she smells of smoke again. Do this periodically so she knows you really mean it. 3) If she does smell of smoke, notify her parents.

Do Not: 1) Do not allow the situation to continue. 2) Do not pretend you don't smell the smoke. 3) Do not accuse her of smoking unless you know for certain that she does. 4) Do not tell the girl's parents without giving her a chance to stop smoking by herself.

Related Problems: 52 Smells of Marijuana.

Problems with Students

◆ 55 ◆
Stealing from the Classroom

Problem: I recently discovered that my wallet was missing from my purse. I strongly suspect one of the boys in my class who has a history of stealing. Some of my students implied that he took it, but they won't say for certain.

Whose Problem: The student's.

Analysis: In addition to a missing wallet, the teacher must resolve a challenge to authority, a crossing of boundaries, and a room of students whose security is threatened.

Do: 1) Confront the child you suspect. Without accusing him directly, let him know that your wallet is missing and must be returned. Emphasize the importance of the return of the wallet. It is expected. 2) Ask the boy if he knows where it might be. Ask him to help you look for it. At some time during the search, walk out of the room for a minute to give him a chance to "find" it or arrange for you to find it. 3) If the wallet is still not found, involve the entire class in looking for it. Be visibly angered and disturbed by the loss. Unfortunately, there is no guarantee that this will work. The more time that elapses after the theft, the less chance for recovery. 4) If the wallet is found, compliment the class. Tell them how sad you feel that the incident happened and that you hope it will never happen again. 5) If the wallet is not found, you have accomplished the following: (a) shown that stealing causes an uncomfortable situation that requires student concern, (b) demonstrated the negative side of stealing—the side of the victim, (c) reminded the class that they are all responsible for each other, (d) reduced the chances that stealing will occur again.

Do Not: 1) Do not blame yourself for leaving your wallet unguarded. 2) Do not refuse to confront anyone because you don't know for sure he or she is the guilty party. 3) Do not directly accuse someone when you don't know for a fact that he or she is guilty. 4) Do not let the focus stray from finding the wallet. 5) Do not offer a reward. It would undermine your expectation of mutual respect in your room and reinforce the act of stealing.

Related Problems: 36 Lying, 56 Stealing from the Community.

◆ 56 ◆
Stealing from the Community

Problem: One of my girls gave me an expensive tie as a Christmas present. After wearing it several times, another student told me the tie was stolen for me. The girl who gave it to me is no longer in our school. I don't know what store it came from.

Whose Problem: The teacher's.

Analysis: It is not certain the student who reported the tie stolen is telling the truth. Because the girl is no longer there to speak for herself, the teacher cannot pursue the truth.

If the tie was stolen, the teacher condones the stealing every time the tie is worn to school. Because the tie has been used several times, it is unlikely the store will want the tie back.

Do: 1) Assume the student who reported the incident is telling the truth. 2) Talk to your class about the incident without mentioning who told you about the theft. Tell them you are uncomfortable wearing a stolen tie. You want them to know that giving stolen items is against the law and not in the spirit of giving. 3) Decide if you are comfortable wearing the tie to places other than school.

Do Not: 1) Do not continue to wear the tie to school. 2) Do not let the incident go without explaining your feelings to the class.

Related Problems: 55 Stealing from the Classroom.

Problems with Students

◆ 57 ◆
Suspected Abuse

Problem: I have a boy in my class who often comes to school with bruises and scratches on his body. I suspect he is being physically abused at home. I also notice that he flinches whenever someone makes a sudden movement near him. I have met his father who seems to be a very aggressive man. I tried to get the boy to talk about his bruises, but he wouldn't complain or admit to anything.

Whose Problem: Perhaps the student's.

Analysis: There may be a number of reasons for the boy's bruises. He may simply roughhouse with his friends and siblings. The father's aggressive behavior does not necessarily mean he is physically abusing his child. Because the teacher has shown interest in the boy, he may still respond at another time if there is a problem.

Do: 1) Report that the boy comes to school with bruises. Report only the facts that you know. It is not justifiable to accuse anyone based only on your suspicions. Your school counselor or administrator will submit the report to the proper authorities. 2) Repeat your concerns to the boy about his bumps and bruises to let him know that you have an interest in him. If there is a time that he needs you, he will come to you.

Do Not: 1) Do not ignore the situation. 2) Do not pump the student for information. If you are making him uncomfortable with your questions he may tell you what you want to hear just to get rid of you. What he tells you may or may not be true. 3) Do not become involved with the family.

Related Problems: 41 Physical Abuse.

♦ 58 ♦
Swearing

Problem: I have a boy in my class who uses a swear word in almost every sentence.

Whose Problem: The student's.

Analysis: It is inappropriate to swear in school. A student who swears is having difficulty with this limit. Either he doesn't understand, or he is testing to see what will happen if he is defiant. In either case he must learn that limits are in place in the classroom and he has to obey them. He must do so not only to prevent his classmates from being subjected to inappropriate language, but also to function properly in society.

Do: 1) Explain that he can no longer swear in your classroom. 2) Have him make a list of the words he feels he should not be using. This will give him an opportunity to be responsible for changing his behavior. 3) Establish a system that penalizes him for using inappropriate words and rewards him for not swearing during given lengths of time. 4) Review his progress daily. 5) Compliment him when he is doing well.

Do Not: 1) Do not allow the situation to continue. 2) Do not swear back to shock him. 3) Do not let yourself become accustomed to this type of speaking. 4) Do not involve the principal or parents. 5) Do not convince yourself that certain people are this way so there is no use in trying to change him.

Related Problems: 32 Insulting the Teacher.

Problems with Students

♦ 59 ♦
Talking Excessively

Problem: There is a girl in my seventh grade class who talks incessantly. I cannot get her to stop.

Whose Problem: The student's.

Analysis: This student has her own agenda. She finds socializing more interesting and important than her schoolwork. There are a number of reasons for this, but they are not the issue. The student must learn to be more attentive and less disruptive in class.

Do: 1) Tell the girl she cannot behave this way in your class. 2) Work out a program together to help her stop talking. Begin by giving her the chance to curtail the talking herself. 3) If she can curtail her talking, be sure to compliment her on her success. 4) If she cannot stop talking, have her work at your desk where she won't have access to other students. Have her face the front and not the class when she is there. She can return to her seat to try again when you feel she can handle it. 5) Should another student approach your desk to talk to her, hold them both responsible and give consequences accordingly. 6) You may also involve her parents in this program by sending home daily reports for them to sign and return to you.

Do Not: 1) Do not scold, nag, or insult the girl when she is not paying attention. 2) Do not ignore the situation or allow it to continue. 3) Do not involve school administration or a disciplinarian unless necessary.

Problems with Students

♦ 60 ♦
Tantrums

Problem: There is a girl in my second grade class who throws a tantrum when she doesn't get what she wants.

Whose Problem: The girl's and her family's.

Analysis A child who throws tantrums in school most likely is getting results by throwing tantrums at home. She must learn that they will not work in school.

Do: 1) When she begins her tantrum move everyone away from her. Tell her she may rejoin the class when she is finished. It may initially take a while, but the tantrums should get shorter when they don't produce the desired effect. 2) If they continue after several weeks, it could be a sign of a more serious problem. In this case ask your school counselor or administrator to approach the subject with her parents.

Do Not: 1) Do not give in to her tantrum. 2) Do not scold or punish her for her tantrum. 3) Do not ask other students to help you stop her tantrum. 4) Do not involve administration unless you suspect a serious problem. 5) Do not talk to her or engage her in any activity while the tantrum is going on.

Problems with Students

♦ 61 ♦
Tardiness

Problem: I have a student who comes late to class almost every day. His tardiness doesn't seem to bother him. I have yelled at him and given him detentions. That doesn't bother him either.

Whose Problem: The student's.

Analysis: It is the student's responsibility to be on time. It is the teacher's responsibility to teach the student and have the lesson prepared when the student arrives.

Do: 1) Tell your student that you are aware of his tardinesses, and it is now time for it to stop. You are not interested in his reasons for being tardy. You are interested only in seeing the problem end. 2) Set up a chart with him to mark the time he comes everyday. This should include a column for the number of minutes he was late. He must show you this chart at the end of class. 3) Reward him for coming on time and/or give consequences for the number of minutes he arrives late. 4) Notify his parents of the plan so they can provide help at home. 5) From time to time at the beginning of class give a five minute quiz for which students lose points if they are not there. 6) If none of these methods work, tell the boy you are sorry he was unable to conquer this problem but hope he will be able to better later.

Do Not: 1) Do not allow the situation to continue. 2) Do not delay class until he arrives. 3) Do not give him time to catch up. 4) Do not get angry or frustrated by him.

Problems with Students

♦ 62 ♦
Tattletale

Problem: A student in my class is always tattling on the other children. Usually she tells me about petty things, but every once in a while I hear something I really should know. I have ambivalent feelings about her doing this.

Whose Problem: The student's, and perhaps the teacher's.

Analysis: A student who tattles may be exhibiting a need to feel close to her teacher. She derives this closeness when the teacher responds with interest to her information. Although the information may be useful, the hardship it can cause the student does not warrant the teacher's encouragement of the behavior. The student may also need to feel a sense of control over students who seem threatening to her. However, her behavior will likely cause the opposite response when the students become angry and threatening because of her tattling. Regardless of her motivation, the behavior is inappropriate.

Do: 1) Discourage the girl from tattling. At the next occurrence tell her it is not a good idea to give you information about other students. Tell her you are concerned the other students will be angry with her. Ask how she thinks the other students feel about her and how she would feel if one of them told something about her. 2) If she is giving you information because she wants to feel close to you, give her a regular classroom task and express your appreciation for her help. Show her that you are more interested in her as a person than in the information she brings you.

Do Not: 1) Do not allow the situation to continue. 2) Do not get angry or punish her for being a tattletale. 3) Do not tell the class what she is doing.

Related Problems: 10 Class Goat.

Problems with Students

♦ 63 ♦
Threatened Abuse

Problem: When one of my students misbehaves, I send a report home to the parents. One boy told me that when he gives his dad the report, his dad hits him. I believe he is telling the truth.

Whose Problem: The student's.

Analysis: The boy may be trying to manipulate the teacher by eliciting sympathy. If his story is true, he must learn how to behave and avoid being punished. He does have control over his behavior, so he can prevent notes going to his dad by behaving responsibly.

Do: 1) Assume you are being told the truth. 2) Tell the boy you won't report to his parents this time. Instead, give him a different consequence so he will understand that he is still being punished. 3) Because this is child abuse, you will have to report it to your administration. Tell the boy you are going to do this.

Do Not: 1) Do not make granting exceptions usual procedure in your classroom. 2) Do not feel you are responsible to protect the boy from his father. 3) Do not neglect to report the incident to your administration. 4) Do not become the boy's ally against his dad—certainly not to the point where you have to change your rules. 6) Do not discontinue reporting about students to their parents.

Related Problems: 41 Physical Abuse.

Problems with Students

♦ 64 ♦
Threatening the Teacher

Problem: One of my students threatened to hurt me if I didn't pass him on a test.

Whose Problem: The student's.

Analysis: A student who threatens a teacher for a grade is a bully with a poor sense of limits and boundaries. He has done two things wrong: used a threat to get something he may not deserve, and acted inappropriately with a teacher. Both of these must be corrected. His threat may or may not be empty. He may not intend to hurt the teacher, but he may do something else destructive, such as damage the teacher's car.

Do: 1) Be just as tough as the bully. Stand firm. Tell him you are going to remember what he said, and report it to your school principal and the police if anything happens. 2) Then back off a little and suggest that he think about what he just said to you. Ask if he is having trouble studying for the test or understanding the material. Can he think of a better way of asking for help than by threatening you? 3) If he asks for help, decide how much you wish to give and what he must do to receive it. 4) Decide whether or not you want to report this incident to the school administrator. If you feel the situation has been resolved and he has learned a better way to conduct himself, you may want to drop the matter. However, if you still feel threatened you should report it.

Do Not: 1) Do not feel intimidated. 2) Do not ignore the incident or fail to follow up on it. 3) Do not try to get even.

Related Problems: 27 Hitting the Teacher.

♦ 65 ♦
Touching the Teacher

Problem: There is a girl in my second grade class who is always touching me. When she stands at my desk she leans against me. She puts her hand in mine when I stand near her, or she comes up to my desk and puts her hand on me. All this touching makes me uncomfortable. Other than this, she is a nice child.

Whose Problem: The student's.

Analysis: A child who is always touching needs physical contact with adults. Either she needs affection or she is afraid of losing the teacher, whom she sees as an important and accepting person. By touching the teacher she makes contact and assures herself that the teacher is still there. However, teachers are not required to give this type of nurturing especially if they are uncomfortable with it. If the student continues touching, a teacher may not want the student around at all.

Do: 1) Tell her privately that she can continue to come up to your desk like everyone else, but should not touch you. Be friendly but firm. 2) Ask her to notice that none of the other students touch you in the ways she does. This will prevent her from feeling that she is the only one who can't touch you. 3) Tell her that there are appropriate ways to touch such as shaking hands with the teacher in the morning. This will give her the physical contact she needs to be "in touch" with you.

Do Not: 1) Do not get angry and push her away. 2) Do not let her continue to touch you if you are uncomfortable.

◆ 66 ◆
Truancy

Problem: A student in my room is often truant. I have spoken to him several times regarding the importance of education and regular attendance, but the situation has not improved.

Whose Problem: The student's.

Analysis: There are several reasons for truancy. Some students may find school work difficult and are trying to avoid it. Some students may simply prefer to be outside. Other students may not see the correlation between their education and future success. They only know that they don't care to be in school now. They are unable to set long-range goals, so school has little or not significance in their lives. The teacher's warnings don't mean anything because students already know high school graduates who still cannot find a decent job.

Do: 1) Contact the school attendance officer and the boy's parents. It is the job of the attendance officer to work with truants and their families. It is the responsibility of the parents to get the children to school. It is then up to you to help him stay in school. 2) Show a personal interest in the student. Set up a series of short term objectives which he can accomplish. This will help him have some feelings of success. 3) Provide a reward each time he reaches an agreed number of consecutive days of attendance.

Do Not: 1) Do not allow the situation to continue. 2) Do not allow the boy to think that he can drop into school whenever he wants. 3) Do not feel that getting him to and keeping him in school is your responsibility alone.

Problems with Students

♦ 67 ♦
Uncontrollable

Problem: There is a boy in my class who is out of my control. He does whatever he wants. His parents will not come to school or talk to me on the phone. My principal told me to take care of it myself.

Whose Problem: The student's and the teacher's.

Analysis: The uncontrollable student has learned that it is better to act out than to be part of the class. It is likely that he is accustomed to having adults angry at him and is trying to draw the teacher into this relationship. There may be nothing the teacher can do for him. However, no one else seems to be willing to help him, and it is the teacher's duty to try. The principal's refusal to take part in resolving this problem causes one of a teacher's biggest nightmares—a difficult student who must be handled alone in the classroom with no support.

Do: 1) Tell the boy you understand that he doesn't want to participate in the class. Let him know that you are sorry he feels this way because there are a lot of things you would like to do with him. 2) Tell him you will respect his feelings by not nagging him, but he must respect the class by not interfering with their work. 3) Assure him that any time he would like to participate with the class, you will be glad to work with him. 4) Look for ways you can include him in class procedure. If you rotate jobs, such as erasing the chalkboard, be sure he is included. 5) Continue to recognize his presence in class. 6) Try to curtail his acting out but do not become angry at him if he continues to do so. 7) Report to your union that your principal has refused to help with a discipline problem and ask what can be done under the terms of your contract.

Do Not: 1) Do not take his actions personally. 2) Do not let him make you angry. 3) Do not give up on him. 4) Do not isolate him from the rest of the class and exclude him from class procedure.

Related Problems: 114 Unsupportive Principal.

Problems with Students

♦ 68 ♦
Whining

Problem: I have a 10-year-old girl in my class who is always whining. I'm sure she is unaware how she sounds because if she were aware, she would stop.

Whose Problem: The student's.

Analysis: Either the girl wants to behave in a regressed way, or she is unaware of how she sounds. A whining voice can be very irritating to others. Not only is the teacher motivated by a desire to help the student, but also by a desire to not hear her whine anymore.

Do: 1) Make her aware of how she sounds. Tell her you would like to tape-record her so she can hear herself. When she listens to the tape, ask her if she wants to change the way she talks. Let her experiment with other ways of talking on the recorder. 2) Invent a signal which will let her know she is whining again. Compliment her while she is improving so she will know that her effort is paying off.

Do Not: 1) Do not allow the situation to continue. 2) Do not get angry and yell at the student because it is bothering you. 3) Do not convince yourself that it isn't important and will go away by itself. 4) Do not whine back at her to show her how she sounds. This will only belittle her and make her less likely to cooperate with you in any program to eliminate the whining.

Related Problems: 58 Swearing.

Problems with Students

♦ 69 ♦
Withdrawn

Problem: I have a young child in my third grade class that is extremely withdrawn. He barely responds to me and seldom does what the rest of the class is doing. I spoke to his parents about this, but they insist he is just a little slow.

Whose Problem: The student's and his family's.

Analysis: There are several reasons for withdrawn behavior, among them—autism, schizophrenia, phobias, retardation, hearing loss, and anxiety. The teacher's concern is not to diagnose the cause, but to acquire the appropriate educational services for the child. Although the child's parents may suspect something is wrong, they may be in denial about their child having a problem that needs to be treated.

Do: 1) Determine the problem by arranging with the parents to have the child tested. If the parents balk, you and your administrator can consider a due process hearing with your board of education to obtain the necessary services for the student. 2) Evaluate how the school system can best serve the student's special needs. 3) With an administrator, address the results of the testing with the parents. Remind them of their child's strengths. Provide support and understanding to the parents as they face their child's problem for the first time. They may feel a sense of relief that the school is prepared to help them.

Do Not: 1) Do not allow the situation to continue without intervention. 2) Do not focus only on the child's shortcomings when dealing with the parents. 3) Do not feel there is nothing you can do to help the child. 4) Do not fail to be supportive of the parents.

Chapter II

Problems with Special Education Students

◆ *Students become special education students when they require special attention to keep up with their abilities.*

◆ *Teachers should not "dumb down" for special education students.*

Problems with Special Education Students

♦ 70 ♦
Depressed

Problem: I have a girl in my classroom who was recently in an automobile accident that left her without the use of her legs. She will always be in a wheelchair. The class and I are trying to be supportive, but she is still very depressed.

Whose Problem: The student's.

Analysis: The girl has a right to be depressed. She recognizes that she will have to make several adjustments in her life. There will be things the other children do which she will never be able to do. She feels different. This, in itself, is often difficult for children to accept. It is likely that she is focusing on all she will be missing.

Do: 1) Continue to be supportive and help the class do the same. 2) Encourage her friends to continue doing things with her. 3) Allow her to be depressed for a while. It will take some time for her to become accustomed to her new situation. 4) Keep her school routine in place. 5) Agree with her that life will be challenging but assure her that you feel she can meet these challenges.

Do Not: 1) Do not treat her as if she is now a problem to the class. 2) Do not tell her that things aren't so bad. The worst thing you can do is to deny her feelings. 3) Do not stress what is now different about her.

Related Problems: 77 Wheelchair-Bound.

Problems with Special Education Students

◆ 71 ◆
Disabled with Discipline Problems

Problem: A girl in my room has asthma severe enough to prevent her from taking PE. The faculty was told by the principal not to confront her, even if she misbehaves, because stress may cause her to have an asthma attack. She seems to take advantage of this situation by misbehaving without concern for consequences.

Whose Problem: The student's.

Analysis: This is a control issue. The girl is using her disability to manipulate the teachers. It is likely she uses the same tactic at home. Her asthma may even be psychosomatic.

If the teacher were to risk a confrontation with the student, she would probably have a severe attack and require hospitalization. The teacher's subsequent guilt would prevent her from ever confronting the girl again.

Do: 1) Arrange a meeting with the girl, her parents, and perhaps one of your school administrators or the school counselor. 2) Tell them you are uncomfortable with the present situation. You feel the girl is not developing the personal responsibility that the other students are developing. She must learn that preventing her asthma attacks is her responsibility. She must follow the same rules that the rest of the class follows and realize there will be consequences if she does not. 3) Make it clear that she needs to work on her good behavior in order to avoid situations that might result in a confrontation. 4) If she is to be confronted, develop a procedure to follow which would not cause her to have an asthma attack. Point out that she must learn to deal with confrontations, because they are a part of life.

Do Not: 1) Do not allow the situation to continue. 2) Do not feel that preventing her asthma attacks is solely your responsibility. 3) Do not feel that if she has an attack it is your fault. 4) Do not allow her to control you.

Problems with Special Education Students

♦ 72 ♦
Grading

Problem: I am a special education teacher for students with behavior disorders. I grade my students on a different standard than the one used by the rest of the school. My students get A and B grades if I feel they are trying hard or showing improvement. This encourages them. Some of my colleagues say my students should be graded the same way as the rest of the students in the school.

Whose Problem: The special education students'.

Analysis: Some teachers feel all students cannot be measured by the same criteria. In their view, a grade is a message. If the student is doing better, his grade goes up. If he is doing worse, his grade goes down. Others feel there is a standard, and the students' grades should reflect how well they have done against this standard. Either of these methods would be all right if everyone in the school used the same one. However, a school cannot use both at the same time. How would students, parents, college registrars, or prospective employers know which concept was used? How would administrators know if the student was doing well enough to return to mainstream classes? It is better to use the same grading standard for everyone. Not only is it less confusing, it is also more honest.

Do: 1) Work with your school administration to decide how special education grades are to be given and develop one policy everyone uses. 2) Make parents aware of this policy. 3) Find other ways of rewarding improved work.

Do Not: Do not use grades for anything other than a measure of academic success.

Related Problems: 75 Parties.

Problems with Special Education Students

♦ 73 ♦
Inclusion

Problem: As a part of the inclusion program in my school I am getting a student who is blind. I don't know what to expect from her or what additional work I will have to do.

Whose Problem: The principal's.

Analysis: Proponents of inclusion are quick to point out its many benefits for the student. However, inclusion presents some problems as well. Many administrators push inclusion, often for financial reasons. Many social agencies push inclusion in hopes of providing equal opportunities for their clients. Often in such cases, procedures helpful to their clients have not been adequately worked out. Regular classroom teachers may be apprehensive about receiving special needs students because they don't know what to expect or how to meet the exceptional student's special needs.

Before a student with special needs can be given special education services of any kind, there must be a staffing for everyone concerned. This would include the principal, the special education representative, a nurse, the parents, the student, and the receiving classroom teacher. This is known as the multi-disciplinary staffing. At this time the abilities and limitations of the student will be discussed and plans will be made for teachers and ancillary staff to work with the student.

Do: 1) Attend the multi-disciplinary staffing. As the receiving classroom teacher, you will be the one to carry out the educational plan. This staffing must make clear what all involved persons are to do. 2) Freely express your abilities as well as your limitations in working with this student. 3) Discuss your responsibilities in collaborating with the ancillary staff. 4) Inform your union of the need to work with the board of education to establish guidelines for regular classroom teachers working with students who have special needs.

Do Not: 1) Do not think a special needs student has nothing to gain from being in your classroom. 2) Do not feel you have nothing to offer a special needs student. 3) Do not accept the student without clear understanding of the expectations for her. 4) Do not

Problems with Special Education Students

accept a student if you don't feel qualified to provide the services needed from you. 5) Do not accept a special needs student if you cannot be assured you will receive the support necessary to provide a good education.

Related Problems: 74 Learning Disabilities.

Problems with Special Education Students

♦ 74 ♦
Learning Disabilities

Problem: I am getting a student with learning disabilities. The principal said I should modify his work and the expectations I have for him. I don't know exactly what I should do.

Whose Problem: The principal's.

Analysis: Students with learning disabilities make up the largest portion of special education. Many of them are now going into mainstream and inclusion programs. They have a good chance of being successful in the regular classrooms if the teachers understand the students' needs and how best to meet them.

If the teacher is unsure of how to work with a learning disabled student, the principal has not provided enough information about the student's needs. Learning disabilities consist of a multitude of learning problems. Each can be handled in a multitude of ways. If the child needs much of his work adapted, he should be given an aid or go into a learning disabled program. A principal who expects a teacher to modify large quantities of work for one student may be trying to avoid hiring a special education teacher. The regular classroom teacher is then required to do extra work. This is not what inclusion or mainstreaming was meant to be.

Do: 1) Initiate a multi-disciplinary staffing with you, as the classroom teacher, included. Determine the student's learning strengths and problems. Establish the most effective methods of meeting his needs. 2) If extensive adaption of classwork is required, request an aid. The concept of special needs students in the regular classrooms is that they will be doing as much of the regular work as possible with as many of the normal expectations as possible.

Do Not: 1) Do not develop a negative attitude toward the student. 2) Do not take on an entire set of new responsibilities without help. 3) Do not allow a special education student into your classroom without receiving specific information about the student and his abilities. 4) Do not allow a special education student into your classroom without being present at or seeing the results of the planning meeting.

Related Problems: 73 Inclusion.

Problems with Special Education Students

♦ 75 ♦
Parties

Problem: We have a special education room for behavior disordered students who attend our school. Every Friday they have a pizza party and a video movie. The students in my room have been asking for parties and video movies too.

Whose Problem: The special education program's.

Analysis: A special education teacher who has weekly parties is attempting to reward students for reaching certain goals during the week. Parties may be part of a formal rewards program or merely a way for the teacher to connect with students and make school seem more positive.

However, such a program presents several problems. The party takes about 10% of the learning time away from special education students, who are often behind in their learning and need every minute of instruction they can get. The weekly rewards may encourage students to remain in special education when the program should be encouraging students to return to the mainstream classroom. Weekly parties in the special education classroom also create a desire for other classes to want parties.

Do: 1) Speak with the special education teacher and see if he intends to continue the parties. Let him know the problems they are causing. 2) Encourage the special education teacher to find other ways of rewarding his students. Perhaps having a pizza party when a student is main-streamed would be more appropriate. 3) If he does not offer to change his policy, meet with him and your local school problem committee to voice your concerns again.

Do Not: 1) Do not tell your class that the special education students get treats because there is something wrong with them. 2) Do not start having weekly treats and parties in your room. 3) Do not become angry with the special education teacher.

Related Problems: 134 Students Invited to Teacher's Home.

Problems with Special Education Students

◆ 76 ◆
Retarded

Problem: My principal will soon place a girl with a low IQ in my sixth grade class. To keep up with the rest of the children, the girl will require a great deal of my attention. I don't think this is fair to me or the other students.

Whose Problem: The student's and the principal's.

Analysis: Students with low IQ's are mainstreamed for several reasons. The principal may feel the student needs help socializing in a normal setting or that she is capable of keeping up with the rest of the class. In either case these goals must be made clear to the teacher.

Do: 1) Ask the principal what the expectations are for this student. 2) Find out if there is any support for you, such as an aid or a resource program. 3) Determine what her parents expect her to do. 4) Learn about the student's strengths. 5) Plan some group work so she will have additional support. 6) Have other students give her help from time to time. 7) If the girl is still unable to meet the stated goals, request to have her considered for special education services.

Do Not: 1) Do not try to meet unrealistic expectations. 2) Do not spend so much time with this student that it takes away from the rest of the class. 3) Do not feel you are the only person responsible for this student.

Related Problems: 51 Slow Learner, 73 Inclusion.

Problems with Special Education Students

♦ 77 ♦
Wheelchair-Bound

The Problem: I will soon be getting a student who is physically disabled. She is in a wheelchair. I am not sure what she can and cannot do. I am embarrassed to ask because I don't want to upset her with a lot of questions.

Whose Problem: The teacher's.

Analysis: Although a student in a wheelchair may be a new experience for the teacher, it is not a new experience for the student and her family. They are accustomed to answering questions and will not be upset.

Do: 1) Meet with the new girl and her parents. Be open with them. They will not feel that your questions are inappropriate if you show your desire to create a good learning environment for the girl. 2) Discuss some of the activities she will be doing in your class. Ask if she needs any special accommodations in order to participate. Ask if she would like one of the students in the room to be a helper. You could let her pick someone or let each student have a turn. This would help the girl and give the other students the chance to work with a friend who has special needs. 3) Keep in mind that she is in your room to have an educational experience that is as normal as possible. It is most important that the girl feels she is part of the class.

Do Not: 1) Do not be embarrassed. 2) Do not feel at a loss as to what you should do. 3) Do not feel you always have to make special provisions for her. 4) Do not emphasize her differences.

Chapter III

Problems with Yourself

♦ *The teacher is the center of the classroom.*

♦ *There are some people who say they can do it, and there are some people who say they cannot do it, and all of them are correct.*

♦ *Have reasonably high expectations.*

♦ *Those who don't expect very much will not be disappointed.*

Problems with Yourself

♦ 78 ♦
Accused by Student

Problem: A student accused me of hitting her. I was told not to come to work until the matter could be settled. I didn't do this to her, and I feel I am being treated unfairly.

Whose Problem: The teacher's.

Analysis: Although this is a difficult situation, procedures have finally been adapted which insure both the safety of the child and the rights of the accused. In many cases a child who unjustly accuses a teacher of abusive misconduct does not understand the enormity of the accusation. She was angry and wanted to get even, she was curious to see what would happen and couldn't back out, or she meant it as a prank and it got out of hand. The child gets a lot of attention and little or no punishment if it was a lie. The teacher is left with emotional scars, huge legal fees, and a damaged reputation.

If the accusation is true, the teacher will be afforded due process under the law but will most likely lose his teaching position. Teachers who are guilty of abuse hurt not only the child and themselves, but the entire profession.

Do: If you are innocent: 1) Assure the principal that you have done nothing improper. Demand your rights. You are innocent until proven guilty. You may be removed from your class. Depending on the local laws and school contract you have with your board of education, many districts will provide you with office work at your regular salary until your hearing. 2) Notify your union. 3) Contact a lawyer.

If the child retracts her accusation: 1) You should be permitted to stay at your school if that is what you wish. 2) If you feel it is necessary, request the accusing student be transferred to another school. 3) Ask the school to publicize that the child left because of falsely accusing a teacher. 4) If the school is not willing to publicize the false accusation, consider legal action against the family of the child. Ask the parents to be responsible for your legal fees. 5) Consider confronting the child to tell her she has done a very bad thing. 6) Ask the school to administer serious consequence for her behavior.

If you are guilty, resign your position.

Problems with Yourself

Do Not: 1) Do not panic. 2) Do not try to get back at the accuser. 3) Do not resign your position if you are innocent. 4) Do not try to handle this alone. 5) Do not think this can happen only to someone else. 6) Do not answer questions without legal representation.

Problems with Yourself

♦ 79 ♦
Advancing in Teaching Career

Problem: One problem with being a teacher is that the only way to advance is to leave the classroom and go into administration.

Whose Problem: This might be a problem with the profession.

Analysis: For a long time it has been true that the only way to advance in education was to become an administrator. Today there are some ways to advance yourself but still remain in the classroom. Many schools have positions of department chair or section chair. You can exercise leadership by being the school's union representative. Often, especially in a large union, you can advance quite far while remaining in the classroom. Some school systems have adopted an intern program for new teachers. This requires the use of mentor teachers, which is another opportunity for advancement. In addition, every school has its leaders who, although not formally recognized, still acquire status and appreciation. Though this may not translate into better pay, it does make for higher self-esteem and job satisfaction as well as more job security.

Do: 1) Find the opportunities in your school for advancement. 2) If there are no opportunities in your school, consider transferring to a school that has opportunities. 3) Look beyond your school and in your community where there are often ways to enhance your teaching status.

Do Not: 1) Do not feel that teaching allows no place to advance. 2) Do not get into a rut.

◆ 80 ◆
Anger

Problem: Sometimes my students get out of control and don't do their work. At these times I get so angry that it is hard for me to control myself.

Whose Problem: The teacher's.

Analysis: Teachers are in the classroom to present their students with learning opportunities. Whether or not the students take advantage of these opportunities is their decision. If the students decide not to learn, it should not cause the teacher to be angry. The classroom is not a place where students and teachers are pitted against each other. If the teacher is often angry, something outside of school could also be the cause, but the anger is coming out in school.

Do: 1) Determine the source of your anger. 2) If the source is the students' inappropriate behavior, determine consequences that will improve their behavior so they can proceed with their learning. Encourage your students to benefit from the classes. 3) If the source of your anger is outside the classroom, explore options for dealing with your anger. The local board of education or union often have counseling programs specifically for teachers who have feelings of anger and frustration similar to yours.

Do Not: 1) Do not take the actions of the students personally. 2) Do not feel it is you against them. 3) Do not feel angry about their inappropriate behavior.

Related Problems: 82 Controlling Class, 85 Hate Teaching, 94 Trouble Sleeping.

Problems with Yourself

♦ 81 ♦
Bored with Job

Problem: I find that teaching is getting boring.

Whose Problem: The teacher's.

Analysis: Being bored by teaching is not entirely bad. It shows that the teacher's mind is alive and wants to be enriched. The teacher need only recognize this and act on it. A large number of work absences are caused by bored employees who want a break from the routine. Some recognize they are bored and take "mental health" days. Others, who can't do this, get sick in order to stay home. Those who find their jobs interesting don't face this situation.

Do: 1) Try to improve your job situation. Sponsor an extra-curricular activity. Teach a grade level or a class you have never taught before. Take a college course which will enhance your teaching. Get involved in union work. Teach an evening class at a local university. 2) If none of these options resolve your boredom, you may want to consider another area, such as counseling or administration, or another field altogether. If you are bright enough to be bored, you are too good to stay bored.

Do Not: Do not accept your boredom.

Problems with Yourself

♦ 82 ♦
Controlling Class

Problem: I have a number of students in my class who misbehave. It is very difficult for me to control them.

Whose Problem: The teacher's.

Analysis: Much of teaching depends on having the class under control. In a well-behaved class the teacher is usually clear about setting limits and boundaries. Students constantly test these limits and boundaries, and a good teacher constantly reminds her students how they are expected to behave. Students often misbehave only because they don't know what the correct behavior is supposed to be. They must discover that there is acceptable behavior and unacceptable behavior. They must learn to distinguish between the two and act accordingly. Most importantly the students must understand that it is to their benefit when the class runs well. The best control comes not from the teacher, but from the class itself.

Do: 1) Analyze how you come across to your students. Do you give that "look" to the student who is talking out of turn? Do you communicate to your class that they must pay attention? Do students who misbehave get punished consistently? Do you expect the students to exhibit personal responsibility? Do you encourage mutual respect among the students? 2) Arrange to videotape yourself teaching your class or ask a colleague to observe you and make comments. 3) Determine consequences for those students who act inappropriately and rewards for those who are behaving well. 4) Handle misbehavior firmly. A student unaccustomed to punishment will often attempt to talk you out of it. 5) Make the students aware that you are all working together to learn and succeed. You are on their side in this effort. 6) Inform your administrator of your plans to tighten discipline in your classroom. Ask for backup, such as sending problem students to the office. 7) If possible get a parent to help you, even if it is just to monitor a student being given a "time out" in the hall.

Problems with Yourself

Do Not: 1) Do not allow the situation to continue. 2) Do not be passive about maintaining control. 3) Do not try to bully your students into behaving. 4) Do not feel that all discipline has to come from you.

Related Problems: 132 Rules.

♦ 83 ♦
Crush on a Student

Problem: I am a high school teacher. There is a girl in one of my classes who I find very attractive. I think about her quite often. Sometimes I imagine what it would be like to go on a date with her. These thoughts are making me uncomfortable.

Whose Problem: The teacher's.

Analysis: This is a surprisingly common problem and not necessarily a serious one. When a teacher has a crush on a student, it is usually kept a secret and the crush eventually goes away. The teacher and student are most likely distant in age, maturity and interests, resulting in little chance of a successful love relationship. They have a professional relationship founded on trust. It cannot be changed without causing problems.

Do: 1) Imagine yourself with this student at a gathering of your friends. Would she fit in? How would you feel about going to a party with a student? What would it be like to be invited to one of her parties? 2) Realize that this is merely a physical attraction which cannot develop. 3) If the crush does not go away, seek professional advice to resolve it.

Do Not: 1) Do not feel guilty for having these feelings. 2) Do not act on your feelings. To do so would be a betrayal of the trust you were given as a teacher and could also cause damage to the teaching profession.

Related Problems: 78 Accused by Student.

Problems with Yourself

♦ 84 ♦
Ethnic Prejudice

Problem: I have noticed that one group of ethnic students in my class tends to do better than the other students.

Whose Problem: The teacher's.

Analysis: When one ethnic group dominates over others in a classroom, especially if it is the teacher's ethnic group, there is a problem. It is up to teachers, as professionals, to see that their prejudices do not interfere with the services they deliver to their students. Intelligence and talent are equally distributed among all peoples but may not be equally nurtured. The teacher must provide that equal nurturing. If a teacher feels otherwise, there is a good chance the method of teaching will be affected.

Do: 1) Realize that you are a highly trained professional who should recognize special abilities in all children. 2) Give each child the nurturing he or she needs.

Do Not: 1) Do not marvel at the disparity. 2) Do not nurture the disparity.

Problems with Yourself

♦ 85 ♦
Hate Teaching

Problem: I have only a couple of years to go before I can retire and get my pension. Lately I have begun to hate my job so much that I don't know if I can reach my retirement date.

Whose Problem: The teacher's.

Analysis: The teacher is burnt-out.

Do: 1) Resolve that you will make it to your retirement date. 2) Devise a strategy to help you reach it, which could include:
  a) Figure the exact number of days you have left. Subtract the holidays and sick days. This should bring the total down to a number that seems more manageable.
  b) Tell your principal you are having some health problems. Ask if it is possible to be relieved of extra duties which are stressful. Offer to do something less stressful in its place.
  c) Use your sick days one at a time when you feel the pressure mounting. See how many days you can go without using one.
  d) Don't use lunch time for complaining. Eat with people who are fun. Have good food. Enjoy your lunch.
  e) Do a good job on your lessons. Develop some new material. Take satisfaction in the work you present.
  f) Reward yourself on payday with a treat. You have just finished another chunk. You deserve to celebrate.
  g) See if your school district or union offers any kind of counseling, particularly group counseling. If not, check with your medical plan.
  h) If your problems and unhappiness persist, use your sick days to look for other work.

Do Not: 1) Do not view your remaining time as one insurmountable obstacle. 2) Do not dwell on your misery. 3) Do not teach poorly.

Related Problems: 80 Anger, 94 Trouble Sleeping.

♦ 86 ♦
Helping a Student with Personal Problems

Problem: I have a girl in my class who has many personal problems. She often stays after class to talk to me. I feel I can help her resolve a lot of these problems.

Whose Problem: The teacher's.

Analysis: A student with personal problems may sometimes need a sympathetic ear. A teacher can provide this if comfortable with the role. However, meeting with one student several times amounts to attempting therapy, which has pitfalls and problems only a person trained to do therapy would foresee. If the teacher does not have this training, there is a chance the student will be done more harm than good. The teacher's counseling may deter the student from getting needed professional help or undermine the work of the student's current therapist, if there is one. It would not be surprising if a student receiving counseling from a teacher suddenly turned in anger against the teacher, thus damaging the teacher/student relationship.

Do: 1) Contact your school counselor. She would know what this student needs and how to help her find it. 2) Support the student in whatever way she chooses to work on her problem. 3) Maintain your teacher/student relationship.

Do Not: 1) Do not encourage the student to see you on a regular basis. 2) Do not ask leading and probing questions. 3) Do not get involved in the student's personal problems. 4) Do not give up your role as teacher.

Problems with Yourself

◆ 87 ◆
Home Phone Number

Problem: One of my high school students called me at my home to verify his homework assignment. I was stunned. I have an unlisted number, which I never give out to students. When necessary, I will call students' parents from my home, but this is something I control.

Whose Problem: The teacher's.

Analysis: Most teachers have unlisted numbers so they will not be subjected to crank calls. However, there are several ways a student can get a teacher's home phone number. A careless colleague may leave the number lying around. A clerk may leave it on an unattended desk. Today many households have Caller I.D., which would show the teacher's name and home phone number if a call were made from the teacher's home.

Do: 1) Discuss the situation with your staff, reminding them to be careful with private information. 2) If you wish to continue calling parents from your home, dial *67 before dialing the number. This will prevent your number from appearing on the Caller I.D. 3) Quietly take aside the student who called you and tell him nicely, but firmly, that he is not to call you at your home. 4) If you get no more student phone calls at your home, consider that the matter has been resolved. 5) If you get more calls, especially crank calls, you may have to change your number.

Do Not: 1) Do not neglect to dial *67 before you dial a student's number when you are calling from your home. 2) Do not feel that one of your colleagues was responsible for a student getting access to your home phone number. 3) Do not change your number before you know it is necessary.

Problems with Yourself

◆ 88 ◆
Personal Crisis

The Problem: My husband is in the hospital with a serious illness. He will be there for a couple of weeks. I can't teach my classes without thinking about him. My students must suspect something is wrong, but I don't feel I should burden them with my personal problems.

Whose Problem: The teacher's.

Analysis: Teachers often have the misconception that they must do all the giving, while the students do all the taking. On the contrary, several good things may happen if a teacher shares an occasional personal crisis with the students. It will relieve some of the teacher's pressure about the crisis and save the teacher from worrying about the students' feelings. It will teach the students not to be afraid of adversity and demonstrate that life has its bad times that we all go through and survive. It will give the students an opportunity, essential to their growth, to be nurturing and supportive.

Teachers may also mistakenly feel that they must keep their private lives separate from their professional lives. If a teacher keeps secret a personal crisis, the students may sense something is wrong. Without knowing the cause, they may wrongfully blame themselves for the teacher's distractions. It is all right to reverse roles for a little while, until the teacher's husband is well.

Do: Tell the students about your husband.

Do Not: 1) Do not let the students continue to worry about what is wrong with you. 2) Do not stay home to avoid them.

Problems with Yourself

♦ 89 ♦
Personal Politics

Problem: During the last presidential election my students asked for whom I was going to vote. I felt it was wrong to tell them about my personal politics. A colleague of mine doesn't agree with me and freely tells his class how he votes.

Whose Problem: The teacher's.

Analysis: Students often display an interest in politics during an election. They are also interested in their teacher's voting preferences because they are interested in their teacher as a person. Some schools prohibit teachers from discussing their personal political preferences with the students. In other schools that allow it, teachers generally agree not to do so anyway. However, the United States is a democracy whose principles are based on free elections. Ideally, personal choices are reached through political discussion. It is important that children learn this so they will vote intelligently when they reach voting age. If students display an interest in the elections, it is the best time and place to teach them the importance of political discussion.

Do: 1) Unless your school has a specific prohibition about discussing politics, discuss your preferences freely. Explain how you came to your decisions. 2) Teach your students that politicians should stand for certain ideas, and that they should support the candidates whose ideas are the closest to their own. 3) Study the major candidates with your students. Compare and contrast their ideas. Identify those that don't seem to have any. 4) Encourage your students to discuss their own beliefs.

Do Not: 1) Do not tell your students that politics does not belong in school. This only separates school from the real world. 2) Do not bully your students into agreeing with your views or your candidates. 3) Do not make you students feel something is wrong with them if they don't agree with you. 4) Do not give your students a negative view of politics.

Related Problems: 90 Personal Values.

Problems with Yourself

♦ 90 ♦
Personal Values

Problem: One of my students asked me what I thought about abortion. I started to explain but became emotional and gave a much longer answer than I should have. Now I feel guilty about imposing my personal values on the class.

Whose Problem: The teacher's.

Analysis: There is nothing wrong with sharing personal values with students. It is an appropriate part of a teacher's role. Personal opinions are formed in part by listening to the opinions of others. Teachers cannot refrain from being a part of this process, unless they are willing to let everyone except themselves play a part in forming their students' opinions. Other teachers in the school are most likely sharing their values, which are probably not completely in agreement. By hearing several opinions students can form their own values.

Do: 1) Inform your class when you are stating a personal opinion rather than a fact. 2) Give them an opportunity to state their views on the subject. 3) Emphasize forming of opinions, not opinions in particular.

Do Not: 1) Do not tell your students you cannot respond to their question. They might feel that their question is not worth answering, that they are not worth answering, or that you don't know anything about the subject. 2) Do not tell your students that they may not discuss values in school. This separates school from the real world. 3) Do not force your values on your students. 4) Do not make your students feel something is wrong if they disagree with you.

Related Problems: 89 Personal Politics.

♦ 91 ♦
Praise

Problem: I have a student who is very poor in academics. I would like to encourage him with praise, but it is hard to find anything good to say.

Whose Problem: The teacher's.

Analysis: Praise is an essential component of building a student's self-esteem. However, if a student's work is not good, the teacher is left with two options: praise work which was easy to do, or praise work which hasn't been done well. If the teacher praises work that was easy to do, the student may realize he has nothing else worthy of praising. This can only make him feel worse. If the teacher praises work that hasn't been done well, the student will either know the teacher is lying or believe he is doing good work and doesn't have to try harder. If he later discovers he hasn't been doing well, it will not only hurt his self-esteem, but also his trust in the teacher.

Do: 1) Tell the student you feel a person with his abilities should be doing better. Ask if he would like to do extra work to help him improve. 2) If he shows improvement, praise the improvement. Encourage him to continue his effort. 3) Praise him for trying harder than before. If he tries harder but doesn't do any better, praise his effort. Let him know how important it is to try hard and that people appreciate a person who does so. 4) If necessary, give an easier test or assignment so he can experience some success. 5) If you find that he is not trying any harder, accept that he doesn't deserve praise. 6) Let him know that the only way he can get praise is by accomplishing something you both feel good about.

Do Not: 1) Do not feel that students have the right to praise. 2) Do not praise what is trivial. 3) Do not give false praise.

Related Problems: 72 Grading.

♦ 92 ♦
Punishment

Problem: Sometimes I have to punish my students for misbehaving. I have ambivalent feelings about this.

Whose Problem: The teacher's.

Analysis: Punishment is often perceived as something bad and the person giving it as someone evil. When students demonstrate they have not learned how to behave properly, it is the teacher's job to correct their behavior. Punishment is a way of teaching students they have done something wrong when other ways of reaching them have not been effective.

Punishment should have three qualities. It should be logical, remedial, and instructional. Many times removal from class or confiscation of a distracting object is an appropriate punishment. Telling a student he can't go with the class on a field trip is a good punishment for a student who has trouble behaving in public, but is not good for a student who neglects to do his homework. That student should be punished by having to do his homework during his lunch. At the end of the punishment, the student should know a better way to behave.

Do: 1) Determine whether the student's inappropriate behavior can be corrected with punishment. 2) Punish when it is the only way the student can be instructed.

Do Not: 1) Do not punish to hurt. 2) Do not punish if there are other ways of correcting the student. 3) Do not punish to make yourself feel better. 4) Do not punish in a way that has nothing to do with the infraction.

Problems with Yourself

♦ 93 ♦
Successful Teaching

Problem: I would like to feel that I am a successful teacher, but I'm not sure what a successful teacher is or what I must do to become one.

Whose Problem: The teacher's

Analysis: Many teachers attempt to achieve success by progressing with their students as much as they can on their lessons each day. A better approach to successful teaching is to begin with a vision of the whole student and how the teacher and the lessons fit into the students' lives. This is carried into a realistic picture of what the students can accomplish.

Do: 1) Formulate a game plan before the semester begins. 2) Set class goals of what you expect your students to achieve. Have high expectations. 3) Though you may have to make some alterations during the year, try to stick to your goals. 4) Push your students towards these goals by reminding them of their success.

Do Not: 1) Do not feel your teaching is unrelated to all the other teaching a student receives. 2) Do not lose sight of the part you play in an individual student's education. 3) Do not start a class without a strong idea of what you expect the class to accomplish. 4) Do not become discouraged to a point where you greatly lower your expectations (dumb down).

Problems with Yourself

◆ 94 ◆
Trouble Sleeping

Problem: I am so troubled by my students' lack of success and poor behavior that I can't fall asleep at night.

Whose Problem: The teacher's.

Analysis: The classroom should provide opportunity for students to succeed. If students are not succeeding it could be due to the way the teacher is teaching, a lack of participation by the students, or both. It is a problem to be solved, not one to lie awake about.

Do: 1) If possible take some time off from work to evaluate your situation and attempt to overcome your bad feelings. 2) If you decide the problem lies with the students, explore ways you can get them to be more receptive to your teaching. 3) If your situation does not improve, consider asking for a different assignment, perhaps in a different school. 4) Try to discuss your situation with a friend or colleague. Many school systems and unions offer free or low-cost teacher counseling. 5) Consider taking a college course or a workshop to help you regain your confidence. 6) If these measures don't seem to help, consider leaving the field of teaching. If you are close to retirement, you should do what you can to remain until you are able to qualify for a pension. If you are a new teacher, there is nothing wrong with considering some other profession.

Do Not: 1) Do not allow the situation to continue. 2) Do not become so absorbed by your problems that you have trouble functioning. 3) Do not be afraid to admit you made a mistake in choosing a career. 4) Do not avoid seeking outside help if you cannot solve this problem on your own.

Related Problems: 85 Hate Teaching.

Problems with Yourself

♦ 95 ♦
Wanting to Be Liked

Problem: I learned that whether or not you are liked by your students is unimportant. However, I think it is important. I want my students to like me.

Whose Problem: Perhaps the teacher's.

Analysis: There is nothing wrong with a teacher's desire to be liked by the students, but this cannot become the teacher's goal. Too many teachers conclude that to gain the students' affection, they must always give and not demand too much. Students who are treated this way are likely to respond in a friendly manner but will not necessarily do their work. It is more important to earn a student's respect.

Do: 1) Run your class on the following principles:
    a) Everyone in the class must respect each other;
    b) The teacher is on the students' side;
    c) The teacher provides the students with opportunities to grow;
    d) The teacher provides the class structure so the students can achieve growth.
2) Strive to provide for the needs of your students. They will respond by liking you.

Do Not: 1) Do not overemphasize the importance of your students feelings about you. 2) Do not avoid situations where you have to make demands on your students. 3) Do not try to be the students' friend. 4) Do not make a goal of being liked.

Problems with Yourself

♦ 96 ♦
Worried about Class

Problem: I get worried because my students aren't doing well. When we do our annual testing, their grades are so poor I feel I am a failure for not teaching them better.

Whose Problem: The teacher's.

Analysis: The teacher is not taking the test or having educational scores recorded. The teacher's task is to present the material to the class and to guide them through the experience. The students' task is to learn the material and prepare for the tests. If anyone should be worried, it should be the students.

Do: 1) Accept that the students are responsible for taking the tests. 2) Be certain that you have given them adequate preparation. Help them with their test-taking skills. 3) Stress the importance of the tests. 4) Encourage them to do the best they can. 5) After the tests, reward those who did well. Let them know that you are proud of them when they do a good job.

Do Not: 1) Do not be anxious for your students. 2) Do not feel you are the only one responsible for their results.

Related Problems: 42 Poor School Work, 94 Trouble Sleeping.

Chapter IV

Problems with Colleagues

Teachers who want to be treated like professionals must behave like professionals.

Problems with Colleagues

♦ 97 ♦
Faculty Discrimination

Problem: There is racial and religious discrimination in our faculty. I find it difficult to teach in this environment.

Whose Problem: The faculty's, the administration's, and the students'.

Analysis: Discrimination in school creates an environment of tension and distrust. This is likely to distract the teachers from good teaching. The students become affected by this environment making it more difficult for them to learn. There are three possible circumstances, which can occur concurrently, for discrimination in the school: 1) people are deliberately making prejudicial remarks; 2) people are accidently making prejudicial remarks due to ignorance and insensitivity; or 3) innocent remarks are made but were misinterpreted or misunderstood. If numbers 2 and/or 3 are the cause, the situation can be resolved. If 1 is the problem, the offenders will have to learn to put their personal feelings aside and create a less hostile atmosphere. If a large number of faculty are discriminatory, the situation may be difficult to correct.

Do: 1) Try to find other faculty members who share your feelings and ask them to work with you on resolving the problem. It is best if your group represents a cross section of your faculty. 2) Talk to your principal about the situation and point out the harm it is causing to the school. 3) Schedule a faculty meeting to discuss the problem. Contact your local board of education. They may be able to provide an experienced person to lead the meeting. The meeting should emphasize that school is a place of learning even for the faculty. Participants should be encouraged to articulate their feelings whether they have been the subject or the perpetrator of the discrimination. Separate those acting out of ignorance from those acting out of cruelty. Those who did not know they were being offensive should be taught ways to be more sensitive to their fellow workers. Pressure must be put on those who harbor feelings of discrimination to behave in a professional manner. This includes working productively with people they may not like. Leadership must come from the principal. If the principal is discriminatory or if your efforts fail, seek work elsewhere.

Problems with Colleagues

Do Not: 1) Do not ignore the situation. 2) Do not try to get even if people have hurt you. 3) Do not feel powerless. 4) Do not expect to win over people who are blatantly prejudice. 5) Do not allow this situation to detract from your teaching.

Related Problems: 98 Holiday Party.

Problems with Colleagues

♦ 98 ♦
Holiday Party

Problem: I received a note in my school mailbox that our faculty is having a Christmas party. This will include a grab bag and holiday carols. I am the only person on the faculty who is not a Christian. I do not feel I will be a part of this celebration.

Whose Problem: The party planners'.

Analysis: The people planning the party were either unaware or insensitive to your religious beliefs, but probably meant no harm. Parties before Christmas are common because they celebrate not only the holiday but the holiday vacation, which does involve the entire faculty.

Do: 1) Decline the invitation if the Christian theme makes you uncomfortable. 2) In a non-hostile way tell the party planners how you feel. 3) If you simply wish to enjoy yourself, attend the party and view it as participating in another culture. 4) Consider approaching your social committee about celebrating a festive event in your religion. Volunteer to organize it. This would give your colleagues a chance to learn something about another religion and enjoy another social event.

Do Not: 1) Do not interfere with the party. 2) Do not be hostile towards the party and its planners. 3) Do not be silent because you don't want to appear different.

Related Problems: 97 Faculty Discrimination.

♦ 99 ♦
Inadequate Teacher

Problem: The teacher in the next classroom has difficulty carrying out his duties. He has little control over his students. Either I or someone else has to come in to settle them down and get them back to work. During our preparation time he comes to me almost every day to get help with his record keeping. I didn't mind helping him when he was new, but he should be on his own now.

Whose Problem: The inadequate teacher's.

Analysis: In a good working environment everyone helps each other on occasion. However, a teacher requiring constant assistance is manipulating the faculty and setting a poor example for the students. Those who help the teacher enable the situation to continue. The teacher is getting paid for others' work and using their sense of responsibility to avoid personal responsibility.

Do: 1) Tell the teacher that you will no longer help him. 2) Ask the other teachers to do the same.

Do Not: 1) Do not continue to do his work. It only perpetuates the problem. The teacher will learn to handle his responsibilities better if he figures them out for himself. 2) Do not tell the principal. She probably knows about it already but isn't worried because the rest of you are covering the situation. 3) Do not get angry. Stop participating before this happens.

Related Problems: 100 Older Teacher Having Problems.

Problems with Colleagues

♦ 100 ♦
Older Teacher Having Problems

Problem: There is an elderly teacher in the classroom next to mine. She has lost much of her ability to teach. I have to go to her room a couple of times each week to help her settle the class. Other teachers do this too.

Whose Problem: The elderly teacher's and the principal's.

Analysis: Ideally, working people wish to finish their careers with dignity and a sense of fulfillment. This does not always happen. Some outstay their ability to be productive, perhaps to avoid retirement or to increase their pension benefits. Helping an elderly teacher consistently with work enables the teacher to continue doing an inadequate job. The teacher's students may receive poor quality education and the teacher's colleagues may develop hard feelings towards the teacher. The situation needs to be resolved with tact and gentleness so that the teacher can retire with grace.

Do: 1) Find out if the teacher has plans to retire by the end of the year. 2) If she does, the staff should be encouraged to help her. The principal should reduce her responsibilities and encourage her to use her sick days. 3) If she is planning to stay beyond the end of the school year, she cannot be allowed to work at this level and expect others to cover for her. The principal should talk to her about retiring or insist she carry out her own responsibilities.

Do Not: 1) Do not get angry or disrespectful. 2) Do not feel you have to handle this situation yourself. 3) Do not allow the situation to continue indefinitely.

Related Problems: 85 Hate Teaching, 99 Inadequate Teacher.

Problems with Colleagues

◆ 101 ◆
Poor Student Teacher

Problem: I am training a student teacher who is not doing very well. The students don't respect her and don't learn much when she takes over the class. She is not receptive to my suggestions and avoids contact with me as much as she can.

Whose Problem: The student teacher's and her university's.

Analysis: Some student teachers are slow to learn and others may never learn to teach well. It is the responsibility of the senior teacher to help train the student teacher and the responsibility of the student teacher to learn from the instruction.

Do: 1) Discuss her progress with her in the presence of her supervisor or ask the supervisor to talk to her alone. 2) Continue to help her even if she is not receptive to you. 3) Make concrete recommendations which would be of help to her. 4) If you feel the student teacher is not going to pass, notify the supervisor as soon as you can.

Do Not: 1) Do not stop giving training and advice. 2) Do not try to correct her attitude without her supervisor being present. 3) Do not pass her if you feel she is not ready to teach.

Problems with Colleagues

♦ 102 ♦
Sexual Advance from a Colleague

Problem: One of my colleagues has made several sexual advances towards me. I have repeatedly said no. I resent the continuing overtures.

Whose Problem: The colleague's.

Analysis: Sexual harassment is a sensitive and complex topic compounded by society's inability to clearly define it. It can affect either gender. If a person is blatantly provocative, lewd, persistent or threatening, there is no question that this behavior constitutes harassment. However, if the person is merely insensitive and rude, the issue becomes less clear. It is also possible that the person who was harassed has sent suggestive or ambiguous signals to the other party only to have become outraged when an advance was made.

Do: 1) Say no clearly and firmly to the offender so there is no doubt that you want the inappropriate behavior to stop. 2) If the offender continues say very clearly, "I find what you are saying to be offensive. You must stop. If you do not, I will report it." 3) If the behavior still persists, report it to both your principal and your union representative. Ask your principal what steps he is going to take to make sure this doesn't continue. Demand assurance that you will not be subjected to retribution for making your report.

Do Not: 1) Do not allow the situation to continue. 2) Do not be intimidated. 3) Do not feel you are powerless. 4) Do not fail to confront the perpetrator.

Related Problems: 113 Sexual Advance from the Principal.

Problems with Colleagues

◆ 103 ◆
Stealing from the School

Problem: I saw a colleague stealing some expensive equipment from our school. He doesn't know that I saw him.

Whose Problem: The colleague's.

Analysis: People steal from work for many reasons. They may need money to pay debts. They may be trying to make up for an inadequate salary. They may feel they are getting back at a system which has been unfair to them, or they may just be greedy.

Often thieves rationalize that no one is being hurt by their behavior. In truth, stealing from the school is a betrayal of public trust. It is harmful to the students, who will be denied the equipment they need for their learning. It is harmful to the co-workers, who will bear guilt by association if the theft is uncovered.

It is better for both the offender and the entire school if the witnessing teacher can resolve the problem quietly. If involved, the principal may decide to punish the offender instead of getting restitution. This would not help the offender or the school.

If the offender is stealing because of an addiction, it will be only a matter of time before he is caught again. If the offender is stealing out of anger or greed, the police could become involved and there will be formal charges of a crime. The offender may not seek help without first getting into a crisis situation.

Do: 1) Tell your union delegate what you saw. This will prove helpful if the police ask you to make a statement. 2) Together confront the offending teacher. Tell him the stealing must stop immediately and restitution must be made. 3) If you cannot confront him, write a note to the offender telling him you know about his stealing. Unless he stops and makes restitution, you will inform the principal. If you are comfortable, signing the note will make it more effective. 4) If the stealing does not stop or nothing has been done to replace the stolen items, the principal must be told.

Do Not: 1) Do not allow the situation to continue. 2) Do not pretend you didn't see anything. 3) Do not confront the person alone. 4) Do not make the incident public.

Related Problems: 104 Substance Abuse.

Problems with Colleagues

♦ 104 ♦
Substance Abuse

Problem: One of our faculty members has changed greatly this year. He has become solitary, short-tempered and sarcastic. He doesn't look well. He doesn't join us for lunch anymore. He is often absent or present only half the day. The rest of us have to cover his classes. There are rumors of a drug abuse problem. I think this is correct.

Whose Problem: The colleague's.

Analysis: Though rumors may be untrue, they should be considered when a serious problem may exist. A drastic change in behavior is certainly a cause for concern.

Do: 1) Either you or another staff person, perhaps the principal, should talk to the teacher about his change in personality. He needs to see it is having an effect on his students as well as his colleagues. He should be told that his colleagues are concerned about him and that they care about him. 2) Tell him that help is available. Insurance usually covers therapeutic counseling and drug rehabilitation if it is necessary. Services can also be obtained from the board of education or the teachers' union. 3) If he rejects help, tell him that he is forcing a crisis which could eventually affect his job. If the problem is drug abuse, it could escalate until he has no choice but to get help. 4) If necessary, insist that he get help. 5) Along with the other staff members, refuse to cover his half-day absences which allow him to continue missing work.

Do Not: 1) Do not jump to conclusions about what is going on. 2) Do not continue to enable him to take off half days without accounting for them. 3) Do not withdraw moral and emotional support from him when he needs it. 4) Do not help him cover up the problem by supporting the symptoms.

Related Problems: 103 Stealing from the School.

Problems with Colleagues

♦ 105 ♦
Uncooperative Aid

Problem: I have a teacher's aid in my class. We do not work well together nor do we get along with each other. She does pretty much what she wants with the students. I feel she turns some of them against me. This situation is particularly difficult because she is older than I am and has been at the school longer.

Whose Problem: The aid's, the teacher's or both.

Analysis: A teacher is supposed to be in charge of the classroom and classroom decisions, and an aid is to be the teacher's assistant. If the aid has more experience than a teacher, she may resent this relationship. However, if the need arises, the teacher should not be afraid or ashamed to ask for advice when the aid has more experience in classroom procedure, student relationships, and problem solving. It is very important for the students to see their teacher and their aid working in harmony. If there is discord the students may sense it and misbehave.

Do: 1) Talk to your aid either alone or with a third party, such as an assistant principal. Explain how important she is to you and how much you depend on her. Most of all, emphasize the importance of cooperation. 2) Be willing to seek and accept her advice in areas where the aid is competent.

Do Not: 1) Do not continue to struggle against your aid. 2) Do not try to get the aid in trouble. 3) Do not feel you have to deal with this problem alone.

Problems with Colleagues

♦ 106 ♦
Uncooperative Colleague

Problem: I have asked a colleague several times to help me with a special needs student. She always refuses and says it is not in her contract to do so.

Whose Problem: The principal's.

Analysis: Teachers have their duties spelled out in contracts to prevent administrators from assigning extra responsibilities. Such assignments are particularly difficult in teaching children with special needs. Administrators must realize that inclusion is not meant to reduce the number of special education teachers by distributing the special education work amongst the regular teachers. Administrators must supply the necessary staff to educate the special needs students in their school.

Contracts spell out exactly what teachers are required to do. If a teacher is doing a good job fulfilling the requirements of the contract, the teacher should not be subject to reproach. Though some professionals are willing to do more than the responsibilities detailed in the contract, this cannot be required. Just because one teacher is willing to put forth extra effort, does not mean others must do so. Teachers have different circumstances and different aspirations which should be respected.

Do: 1) Do the work yourself or ask another willing teacher. 2) Ask for a special education aid. 3) If you feel special services for this child are critical and you cannot provide them, ask your principal to reconsider the student's placement in an inclusion program.

Do Not: 1) Do not be angry or vengeful toward the teacher who turned you down. 2) Do not feel it is your responsibility to get services for the child.

Related Problems: 73 Inclusion.

Chapter V

Problems with Administrators

◆ *When having a dispute with the administration, determine what is most important to you.*

◆ *When having problems with an administrator, look to the union for help.*

Problems with Administrators

♦ 107 ♦
Additional Assignments

Problem: My principal asked me to be in charge of reading and math testing for the school in addition to my regular teaching. There is no extra pay for doing this. I don't mind the additional responsibility, but I don't want to feel someone is taking advantage of me.

Whose Problem: The principal's.

Analysis: It is all right to do extra work without extra pay if there is some other reward for the teacher. The project could be a good opportunity for advancement, a chance to prove leadership abilities, or simply an opportunity to be helpful. Although there is no monetary reward, the principal has other ways of rewarding a teacher, such as time off, easier duty or higher status.

Do: 1) Ask what the job will entail:
  a) What will you have to do?
  b) How much time will you have?
  c) Will you have any help?
  d) Will you be relieved from any of your regular duties? and
  e) Will there be recognition for a job well done?
2) If you feel comfortable with the proposal, then accept the assignment.

Do Not: 1) Do not be angry about receiving the assignment. 2) Do not do the assignment without receiving recognition. 3) Do not accept a future assignment if you didn't feel appreciated the first time.

Related Problems: 108 Additional Assignments You Cannot Do.

Problems with Administrators

◆ 108 ◆
Additional Assignments You Cannot Do

Problem: My principal asked me to supervise the school-wide math and reading testing. This is a lot of work and there is no pay for it. I don't know how I am going to handle this. I have a family to take care of. There are only so many hours in a day.

Whose Problem: The principal's.

Analysis: Adults should work to live, they should not live to work. Family should come first. When asked to take on unwanted additional work, teachers should tell the principal in a positive way that the work is beyond their present capabilities.

Do: 1) Tell the principal you feel honored he has chosen you for this task. However, because of family responsibilities it would be very difficult for you at this time. Do not list these responsibilities and avoid using such words as "can't" and "impossible." 2) If the principal insists you are the person best suited, suggest a co-partner and ask to be relieved from some of your regular duties. 3) Demonstrate your lack of willingness by asking a lot of questions about what the job requires and whether certain details are necessary. By this time your principal may begin to wonder if another person might be better suited for this project. If that doesn't happen, you may at least find yourself with some help. 4) Consider saying no if necessary.

Do Not: 1) Do not accept responsibility you cannot handle. 2) Do not do a bad job on purpose. 3) Do not take the job and complain about it. 4) Do not turn down the job if you are looking to advance in your school or hoping to be seen as a leader.

Related Problems: 107 Additional Assignments.

Problems with Administrators

♦ 109 ♦
Curtailed Program

Problem: My fourth grade students were working on a math project in which they collected and interpreted data from their neighborhoods. They were learning practical mathematical concepts and really enjoying the program. The principal told me I should stop this program immediately and use the math text and workbooks.

Whose Problem: The principal's.

Analysis: Although a teacher is correct in employing practical concepts to actively involve the students in learning, the lesson must remain within the boundaries set by the school principal. The principal has the authority in the school. A teacher who fights with the principal or tries to go higher will most likely be the loser.

Do: 1) Speak privately to your principal. Try to make him see your point of view. If he still does not agree with you, discontinue the program. Although this does not seem fair or in the students' best interest, you must do the best job you can under the circumstances. 2) Attempt the project with another class when there is a new principal or the present principal has acquired more trust in your judgement. 3) Consider working with other teachers in your district to gain more control of school policy towards classroom activities.

Do Not: 1) Do not get into a power struggle with your principal. 2) Do not tell the class your principal made you stop the program they liked. 3) Do not go over the principal's head. 4) Do not think there was something wrong with your lesson.

Problems with Administrators

◆ 110 ◆
Grade Changes

Problem: One of my students did not do as well in my class as he did in his other classes. I gave him a C. My principal asked me to change it to a B. I really don't want to change this grade, but I don't want to fight with the principal either.

Whose Problem: The principal's.

Analysis: Most likely the principal is reacting to pressure placed on him by the student's parents. By insisting that the student get a grade he did not deserve, the principal is undermining the teacher's authority. Though the principal may tell the teacher there is good reason for the change, the teacher won't feel any better. However, the teacher's relationship with the principal is more important than the student's grade.

Do: Tell your principal that you understand his situation, but are uncomfortable giving a grade that wasn't earned. You would like to stay out of this. If he wants the grade changed, he should respect your feelings and change it himself.

Do Not: 1) Do not argue with the principal. 2) Do not get angry. 3) Do not give in and develop bad feelings.

Related Problems: 115 Clout.

♦ 111 ♦
Harassment from the Principal

Problem: My principal really gives me a hard time. Nothing big. Just a lot of little things.

Whose Problem: The principal's or the teacher's.

Analysis: A teacher feeling harassed by the principal has three possible causes: a) the principal really is harassing the teacher; b) the principal doesn't realize the effect her actions are having on the teacher; c) the teacher is imagining the harassment.

Do: 1) Arrange a meeting with the principal to discuss your feelings. Consider inviting your union representative, although a third party could prevent your principal from openly discussing her feelings on the subject. 2) Tell your principal what you think is happening. 3) If there is a misunderstanding, the two of you can work it out. The meeting may make the principal more sensitive towards you in the future. 4) If you sense from the principal's response that there has been intentional harassment, attempt to work something out together. 5) If you are unable to resolve the situation, consider transferring to another school or sticking it out if your principal is retiring soon.

Do Not: 1) Do not allow the situation to continue. 2) Do not get angry before you know if you are right. 3) Do not feel you have no control over the situation.

Problems with Administrators

◆ 112 ◆
Lack of Administrative Action

Problem: I was assaulted by a student last week. I reported it to the principal. When I asked to fill out an assault report, I was told by my principal not to blow this out of proportion.

Whose Problem: The principal's.

Analysis: A principal may not want to fill out an assault report because a bad incident will reflect poorly on the principal's leadership. In reality, it is foolish to neglect following up on an assault. It only increases the likelihood that it will happen again. Any reason the principal has for not filing a report is not worth the problems which can develop if the situation is left unresolved. If the teacher does not resolve the incident, the students receive a clear message that it is all right to assault a teacher. The faculty will feel endangered and morale will suffer.

Do: 1) Confront the principal again for the assault form at a time convenient for both of you to fill it out and sign it. 2) Tell the principal you would like to check back in a couple of days to find out the disposition. 3) Ask for a copy with the principal's signature. 4) Inquire about the procedure after the form is submitted. Is there anything you should expect to happen? When will you need to get involved? Is there someone you should call? 5) If he is not willing to take care of your situation while you are there, ask when you can expect some action to take place. 6) Contact your union office to let them know about both the assault and the lack of support from your principal. Ask them for suggestions on how to proceed.

Do Not: 1) Do not let the situation dissolve without taking action. 2) Do not be intimidated by your principal. 3) Do not feel that you are alone in this.

Related Problems: 27 Hitting the Teacher.

Problems with Administrators

♦ 113 ♦
Sexual Advance from the Principal

Problem: My principal called me into the office for what I thought was to be a meeting. I was, instead, sexually propositioned with implied threats of losing my position if I did not submit.

Whose Problem: The principal's.

Analysis: Inappropriate sexual advances made by a principal create a situation more difficult than when a colleague acts similarly. The authority of the principal's position threatens a teacher's job quality and security. It is important that the teacher take action, even if it is uncomfortable to do so.

Do: 1) Contact your union representative and relate what happened. 2) Confront your principal with your representative. State that you are not interested in any relationship other than a professional one. You will file a grievance if a sexual advance happens again or if there are any repercussions from this conversation. 3) Attempt to find other teachers who have had similar incidents with the principal. If you discover such teachers, try to persuade them to take action with you. 4) If necessary, talk to the principal's superiors. Do this with your union's help. Get their advice as to how you should carry out this procedure. 5) Consider asking a friend or relative to advise and support you as you proceed.

Do Not: 1) Do not allow the situation to continue. 2) Do not be intimidated. 3) Do not feel the situation is out of your control. 4) Do not fail to confront the perpetrator. 5) Do not give in to save your job.

Related Problems: 102 Sexual Advance from a Colleague.

Problems with Administrators

♦ 114 ♦
Unsupportive Principal

Problem: I had an unpleasant incident with one of my students. The next day his mother came to school and complained to the principal about me. The principal called me into her office and chewed me out in front of the mother. I didn't even have an opportunity to give my side of the story.

Whose Problem: The principal's.

Analysis: A principal who reprimands a teacher in front of a parent needs the parent's approval for some reason and is willing to sacrifice the teacher's dignity to gain it. The principal needs to be confronted about this lack of support for the staff.

Do: 1) If your school has a professional problems committee, ask that they address the subject of lack of administrative support. 2) Try to view this as a problem that needs to be solved, not a chance to get even. 3) If you prefer, talk to your principal alone and tell her how you feel about this situation. Emphasize that you are uncomfortable about it happening again. 4) If this matter cannot be resolved, learn to live with it or consider working elsewhere.

Do Not: 1) Do not feel that you have no recourse. 2) Do not blame yourself or feel you have lost face. 3) Do not ignore the situation.

Related Problems: 112 Lack of Administrative Action.

Chapter VI

Problems with Parents

♦ *Try to be on the side of the parents. If you can't, remember you are the professional.*

♦ *If you have a student with problems, remember who sent him to school.*

Problems with Parents

♦ 115 ♦
Clout

Problem: I have a student who did so little work in my class this year that he failed the course. His mother is the president of our school council and active in community politics. She told me she wants her son's grade changed so he can pass the course.

Whose Problem: The mother's.

Analysis: This mother may think she is helping her son, but instead she is teaching him that it doesn't matter if he does not complete his work. She is allowing her son to grow up in an unrealistic environment. By pressuring the teacher to change his grade she is keeping her son dependent on her, which may be exactly what she wants. This will create difficulties when it comes time for him to seek employment. It may also hinder his ability to form personal relationships.

A student should fail for not working up to standard. He still needs to learn the work and should not pass until he does. This must be explained to the mother.

Do: 1) Tell the mother you cannot change a grade once it is submitted. 2) Explain that by attempting to have his grade changed, she is increasing his dependence on her and giving him an unrealistic view of what will be expected of him in life. 3) Tell her you are concerned with her son's lack of success and would like him to try again so that he will develop responsibility for himself. 4) If she won't agree, tell her to make her request to the principal. You must then go along with the principal's decision.

Do Not: 1) Do not get into a power struggle with the parent. 2) Do not feel intimidated. 3) Do not argue with your principal over this matter. 4) Do not change the grade yourself.

Related Problems: 110 Grade Changes, 116 Clout Threatened by Student.

Problems with Parents

◆ 116 ◆
Clout Threatened by Student

Problem: I have a student in my sixth grade class whose father is an important politician. This student feels she doesn't have to do any work because I wouldn't dare fail her. She is right. I would get into a lot of trouble at school if I did fail her.

Whose Problem: The student's.

Analysis: The student is avoiding responsibility and engaging you in a power struggle. She is being manipulative because she thinks she can avoid both responsibility and consequences.

Do: 1) Contact the father. No matter how powerful a politician, he is also a father and likely to be concerned with his daughter's progress. Tell him you are concerned that she is not doing her work. Suggest that you notify him of her assignments so he can work with her and see that they are done. 2) If the father is not agreeable, inform your principal of the situation. 3) If the principal insists that you pass the girl anyway, follow the orders despite your frustration. Sadly, the girl will eventually reap the effects of entering the world with limited skills.

Do Not: 1) Do not feel intimidated. 2) Do not give her a grade just because she asked for it. 3) Do not argue with your principal over this issue. 4) Do not argue with the parent.

Related Problems: 110 Grade Changes, 115 Clout.

Problems with Parents

♦ 117 ♦
Considers Child Gifted

Problem: There is a girl in my class whose mother insists her daughter is gifted and belongs in a gifted program. Though the girl is capable, her standard testing and her school work do not indicate that this is appropriate for her.

Whose Problem: The mother's.

Analysis: The mother has expectations which her daughter cannot reach. If the mother is shown her daughter's scores, she is likely to make excuses for her daughter and remain insistent. If the girl is put in gifted classes, she will be forced to struggle under pressure for her mother's sake. It is better that the teacher bear the brunt of the mother's disappointment than make the daughter struggle with work which is above her.

Do: 1) Explain to the mother that you cannot put the girl in accelerated classes. 2) Stick to your decision even if the mother argues with you. 3) If she persists, refer her to the principal for a discussion of your decision.

Do Not: 1) Do not give in to the wishes of the mother. 2) Do not try to compromise with the mother. 3) Do not put the girl in a position where she is the object of the mother's frustration.

Related Problems: 23 Gifted.

◆ 118 ◆
Doesn't Like Child

Problem: I called a parent to discuss her daughter's behavior problems. It became apparent that the mother did not like her daughter. She related several negative incidents and only referred to her daughter in derogatory terms. I felt sorry for the girl and regretted involving her mother.

Whose Problem: The mother's.

Analysis: Sometimes a parent does not like his or her child. It may be difficult for the teacher to understand how a parent could have such feelings. However, it is only necessary for the teacher to acknowledge the existence of these feelings and adjust accordingly.

A teacher is responsible for the student's welfare in school. It is difficult to protect students in the outside world, especially from their own parents, but the teacher must try.

If the teacher tells the parent about a problem the child has, there is a risk of giving the parent ammunition to use later against the child. The child may think the parent and teacher are working together against her. The action may also contribute to the child's perception of herself as a bad person. This perception may be the reason for the girl's behavior problems.

Do: 1) Be careful what you tell the parent. Indicate that any problems the child is having are being worked out. Involve the parent as little as possible. 2) Tell the girl what she does in school is between the two of you. You have confidence in her ability to do well, and you are here to help her. There is a good chance the girl will like this treatment and behave better because of it. 3) Inform her mother only about the good things she does.

Do Not: 1) Do not become a pawn in a battle between mother and daughter. 2) Do not reinforce the girl's feelings of low self-esteem. 3) Do not treat the mother as a partner in the girl's education.

Problems with Parents

♦ 119 ♦
Inappropriate Note

Problem: The mother of one of my students sent me a note that said she would have to take her daughter out of school for a medical check-up. The note paper had an obscene picture printed on the top. I suppose she thought this was humorous.

Whose Problem: The mother's.

Analysis: Though the mother's use of an off-color note pad was probably meant to be humorous, it could also have been a demonstration of her dislike for the teacher or the school. If the teacher does not react to this note, it will tell the mother that it is all right for her to use this kind of paper for school business. The mother's lack of respect could be passed on to her daughter.

Do: 1) Assume the mother doesn't know any better and needs to learn the correct way to send a note. 2) In a brief note of your own, thank her for notifying you and mention that you would prefer future notes be written on paper suitable for school business.

Do Not: 1) Do not ignore the situation. 2) Do not get angry. 3) Do not attempt to get even by sending her an inappropriate note. 4) Do not involve the daughter in this problem.

Problems with Parents

♦ 120 ♦
Overprotective

Problem: There is a boy in my third grade class whose mother overprotects him. Not only does she walk him to and from school, but she watches him at recess from outside the fence. She seems to be around for everything he does.

Whose Problem: The mother's and the boy's.

Analysis: The mother is having difficulty letting go of her son. She is denying him the opportunity to develop his independence and self-responsibility. The boy may like this because it is easier to have someone take care of him than to take care of himself. Sometimes fear of loss and insecurity are very deep and hard to deal with.

Do: 1) Have your school counselor meet with the mother. The counselor should explain that the mother's actions are not helping her son. The counselor should attempt to establish procedures that will allow the boy to develop with the other children without presenting a threat to the mother. The mother may not be able to adjust to the counselor's proposal, but it must be attempted. 2) If the boy is unable to adjust to the new procedures, suggest to the mother that individual counseling for the boy should be investigated.

Do Not: 1) Do not allow the situation to continue. 2) Do not allow the boy to separate or isolate himself from the rest of the class. 3) Do not allow the other students to tease or pick on the boy for his mother's behavior.

Related Problems: 122 Separation Problems.

Problems with Parents

♦ 121 ♦
Seeking Personal Advice

Problem: A student in my room has serious vision problems. Her parents told me they are considering eye surgery. The operation she needs is risky, with a 50-50 chance that the girl's present eyesight will worsen if the operation is unsuccessful. They asked what I thought they should do.

Whose Problem: The family's.

Analysis: The parents are having a difficult time making a decision. The wrong decision could bring them grief and perhaps guilt. If the teacher offers an opinion, the parents will likely take credit if the opinion proves right but lay blame on the teacher if the opinion proves wrong. No matter how much the teacher cares for the child, it is not the teacher's place to offer an opinion on a matter which must be decided by the child's parents.

Do: 1) Listen sympathetically. 2) Tell them you understand the difficulty of their decision. 3) Thank them for their confidence in including you in making their decision. Tell them, however, that you feel this matter must be decided by the family. 4) Ask them to keep you up to date. 5) Let them know you will support whatever decision they make.

Do Not: 1) Do not give an opinion or anything that could be construed as an opinion. 2) Do not get angry at them or feel offended by them for asking.

◆ 122 ◆
Separation Problems

Problem: Parents usually help in our kindergarten class. One of the student's mothers is here almost everyday and constantly hovers over her daughter. I am uncomfortable with this, but the mother is helpful and I need her assistance.

Whose Problem: The mother's and perhaps the daughter's.

Analysis: Some parents, as well as some children, have trouble separating. Their attachment may be very strong and not easily set aside. Separation problems are usually resolved when the child starts school.

The mother's ability to help the teacher is not the issue. The daughter is in kindergarten to learn independence and to develop social skills. This development is difficult when the mother does not allow the child to function without her.

Do: 1) Tell the mother she may volunteer only one day a month. You may have to insist, but you must prevail. 2) When she does come in, have her help other students. 3) Because this type of parent is likely to complain to the school administration, inform your principal about the situation and your action. 4) Be aware that the mother might transfer her daughter to another school where they will allow her to spend more time with her.

Do Not: 1) Do not allow the situation to continue. 2) Do not allow the parent to manipulate the administration into allowing her to come to school more often.

Related Problems: 120 Overprotective.

Problems with Parents

◆ 123 ◆
Textbook Selection Committee

Problem: My principal asked me to serve on our school council's text book selection committee. I felt honored, until I attended the first meeting. The parents argued vehemently about values. The meeting caused bad feelings and very few textbooks were chosen. The parents have split into two factions and seem to be continuing the feud outside the meeting.

Whose Problem: The community's.

Analysis: Teachers should expect more conflicts to occur as more communities decide to include parents in running the schools. Many parents are not interested primarily in the productive operation of the school. They are more focused on pursuing their own interests, presenting their own points of view, and making them both part of the school curriculum. Religion, personal values and politics are the most frequent issues of concern. Parents should understand that exposure to many different ideas is a part of public education. Professional educators are obliged to present many sides of an issue. Parents are not, so it is not surprising they are acting this way.

Do: 1) Stay neutral during the discussions. 2) Attempt to get the two sides to reach an agreement. Point out that no progress is being made when the arguing persists. Remind the parents that the students need books. It is likely books will contain some material they don't favor. However, they can balance that by discussing those issues with their children at home. 3) Play the role of the facilitator instead of taking sides. 4) If you cannot make any progress, ask the parents to consider dissolving the committee and requesting a new committee to be appointed. 5) If they won't do this, consider resigning from this committee.

Do Not: 1) Do not get drawn on to one side of the disagreement. 2) Do not get into a position where a group of parents is angry at you. 3) Do not serve on a committee that is not getting anywhere.

Problems with Parents

♦ 124 ♦
Uncooperative

Problem: I was on hall-guard duty at a door that is not used for entrance to the school. A parent knocked on the door. When I opened it to speak to her, she pushed her way in and refused to go to the office for a pass as required. She continued into the building, ignoring all directions I gave her.

Whose Problem: The parent's.

Analysis: The parent is showing the teacher she has little or no respect for the school. If this does not change, she will pass this attitude on to her children.

Do: 1) Report the incident to the office. 2) If the parent has already gone into the classroom section of the building, go with someone to find her. 3) Insist she go to the office and follow the proper procedure. 4) If she will not cooperate, it may be necessary to call the police. Check with your principal before you do so.

Do Not: 1) Do not ignore the incident. 2) Do not attempt to use physical force. 3) Do not get drawn into an argument or any other unprofessional action.

Related Problems: 126 Yelling.

Problems with Parents

♦ 125 ♦
Uninterested

Problem: We have parents' night four times a year at our school. I notice there are some parents who never come. I phone to ask if they want to see me during lunchtime or before school starts. Most decline. I think they should take more interest in their child's schooling.

Whose Problem: The parents'.

Analysis: Parents are interested in their children's schooling in varying degrees. Lack of attendance at parents' night does not necessarily indicate they are bad or uncaring parents. Foreign-born parents may be intimidated by their poor English or the unfamiliar atmosphere of the school. Uneducated parents may not know how to become involved with their children's schooling and may prefer to let them handle school-related issues on their own. Others may be unable to come due to their work hours or other obligations. And some, unfortunately, may not care about their children or wish to be bothered.

Do: 1) Continue to extend the invitation to all parents to attend parent's night. 2) Let them know it would be all right to bring a friend or their child with them. 3) Encourage the parents to come, but if it is too difficult, consider offering them other times to meet.

Do Not: 1) Do not feel it is your responsibility to get the parents to attend. 2) Do not offer to visit the parents at home, unless a disability prevents them from attending. To do so would be extending yourself far too much for someone who may not be interested in seeing you anyway.

Problems with Parents

♦ 126 ♦
Yelling

Problem: A parent came to see me after class yesterday. He yelled at me repeatedly. I was very uncomfortable and nothing was accomplished.

Whose Problem: The parent's.

Analysis: The parent's behavior was disrespectful and entirely unacceptable. The situation must be resolved or it may happen again. Parents should not be allowed to think that if they are unhappy with the school, they can come in and yell at the teacher.

Do: 1) Ask the parent to return for a conference. If you wish, ask an administrator to be present. 2) Remind the parent that you share a common interest in helping the child. This is your basis for discussion. 3) Should he begin to raise his voice again, break into his yelling and, in a quiet manner, ask if he is there to solve a problem or just to yell at you. If he says he is there to solve a problem, ask him to continue but without yelling. 4) Find out what it is that he wants. Assume that he is there because of something he thinks you did or should have done for his child. 5) Explore with him the possibility that there was an oversight or a misunderstanding. 6) Explain that you are trained to handle situations in a way that will most benefit the children. This is what you had in mind when the incident happened. You hope he sees under the circumstances that this was the best way. 7) Tell him you would like his help in providing follow up on the child at home. 8) If he raises his voice again, and a third party is not present, suggest you both continue the discussion in the principal's office. 9) Should he become threatening, leave immediately and contact your principal or school security.

Do Not: 1) Do not be intimidated. 2) Do not take it personally. 3) Do not let the parent dominate you. 4) Do not feel you are all alone in this. 5) Never allow a parent to think it is all right to yell at a teacher.

Related Problems: 124 Uncooperative.

Chapter VII

Problems with Procedures

When making an exception to a procedure, remember it is easier to get forgiveness than permission.

Problems with Procedures

♦ 127 ♦
Classics in the Inner City

Problem: The chair of our high school English department told us she wants us to teach Shakespere. This is an inner city school, and I feel that Shakespeare has little relevance or appeal to my students.

Whose Problem: The classroom teacher's.

Analysis: One of the reasons Shakespeare's plays and other classics are still around is their appeal to all, including inner city high school students. Stories such as *Romeo and Juliet* and *A Midsummer Night's Dream* are both about teenagers and should be especially appealing to them. Shakespeare wrote about the human condition, human feelings and human behavior. There is no reason to feel this is inappropriate for students. Every student should have the opportunity to experience great art. The language of Shakespeare may seem difficult at first, but if the teacher helps the students with the first few pages, they will catch on easily.

Do: 1) Teach a Shakespearean play to your class. 2) Discuss what relevance it has for them.

Do Not: 1) Do not neglect to teach the classics because you think they have no relevance to your students. 2) Do not deny your students the experience of great literature, art or music.

Problems with Procedures

◆ 128 ◆
Getting and Keeping Attention

Problem: When I do math with my class I call for the answers orally. It's always the same people who raise their hands. Lately I have started calling on people who haven't raised their hands. I want to be sure everyone is paying attention.

Whose Problem: The teacher's.

Analysis: Students choose to do what is most rewarding for them. Those who answer the questions get positive feedback from their teacher and the opportunity to demonstrate their academic ability. Those who don't volunteer to answer are more comfortable not risking a mistake in front of the class. When a teacher calls only on students who raise their hands, the needs of both types are satisfied. Those who don't answer because they have not done the work are able to avoid the work and still write down the correct answers.

By calling on students who have not volunteered to answer, the teacher turns the situation around. The students who want positive feedback by participating are ignored, and the ones who were safely quiet have their comfort threatened.

Do: 1) Try dividing the class into groups of three or four students of different math abilities. Have the students work together on the problems while you walk around to see that everyone is participating. 2) Try to discontinue reviewing all the problems in class. Ask the students to do their own work at their desks and turn it in when complete. During this time you can help those who are having difficulties. Return the work the next day and review the difficult problems with the whole class. 3) Consider allowing every student to work at their own speed and turn in their work as they complete it. When a student finishes an assignment, get him started on the next one. Base grades on the number of successfully completed assignments.

Do Not: 1) Do not employ a system in which some students do not have to complete the work. 2) Do not employ a system where the students don't know what to expect. 3) Do not employ a system which rewards both workers and non-workers equally.

Problems with Procedures

♦ 129 ♦
Over Maximum Class Load

Problem: My class size is at the maximum allowed by our contract. My principal asked if I would take two extra students. Although it would create extra work, I would not like these students to be without a classroom.

Whose Problem: The principal's.

Analysis: It is your principal's job to see that all the students are accommodated in a classroom without going over the limit. The easiest thing for him to do is to put extra students into full classes. This has three effects: it creates more work for the receiving teacher; it reduces the time allowed for individual student help; and it prevents another teacher from getting a job. Everyone ends up on the short end except the principal.

Do: 1) Tell the principal you do not think it a good idea to go over your class-size limit. You are aware that your board and union have worked out a maximum number of students, and you don't feel you should violate the agreement. 2) If the principal insists, call your union and report it.

Do Not: 1) Do not take extra students into your class. 2) Do not get into an argument with your principal.

Problems with Procedures

♦ 130 ♦
Physical Education Grades

Problem: I received the physical education grades from the PE teacher for my seventh grade students. I was shocked to find that the PE teacher had given C's and even D's to some of my best students. This will keep them off the school honor roll. I realize they are not very athletic, but they are good kids and have good attendance.

Whose Problem: The school's.

Analysis: Many teachers feel that PE, music and art, are not important and should be graded on effort and good attendance. These are the "minors" so how important can they be? However, PE., music and art are as important as math and reading. Health, personal fitness and leisure time are important parts of our lives, yet we do little to prepare for them. All classes should be seen as important and graded on accomplishment.

Do: 1) Explain to your students the importance of participating in PE, music and art. 2) Discuss with your colleagues the importance of PE, music and art. 3) Establish criteria by which grades will be determined based on setting and accomplishing goals. 4) Notify the parents that this will be a school policy.

Do Not: 1) Do not view PE, music and art as less important than other courses of study. 2) Do not apply one grading standard for major courses and another for minor courses.

Problems with Procedures

♦ 131 ♦
Program Cuts

Problem: We have to make program cuts in our high school due to a reduced budget. Although I don't like the idea, gym seems the most likely program for the cuts. We could make the gym program shorter without much of a loss. What else can we do?

Whose Problem: The school system's.

Analysis: In an era that emphasizes the importance of education, it is wrong to consider cutting back school programs for any reason, particularly funding. It is the responsibility of the state legislature and school districts to find funding for all programs.

It is also wrong to consider physical education less important than other subjects. High school education should develop skills for adulthood. Most students will engage in athletics, music and art more frequently as adults than in math or science. Yet physical education, music and art are usually the first programs eliminated when funding is low. Schools are usually willing to finance inter-school athletics to build school spirit. They should also be willing to support physical education programs and cultural subjects for the well-rounded education of all their students.

Do: 1) Resolve that there will be no cutbacks. 2) Work with your faculty, the board of education, parent groups and students to see that cutbacks don't take place. 3) Contact your state legislators. Make them aware of the needs of your schools. 4) If the legislators are unable to help you, work with your school group to determine a means to continue the program. 5) If you find a lack of support or interest, consider making cuts in the math and science programs. This should attract more support.

Do Not: 1) Do not feel as though you have no part in this decision. 2) Do not feel that classes such as physical education, art and music are less important than the academic classes.

Related Problems: 130 Physical Education Grades.

Problems with Procedures

♦ 132 ♦
Rules

Problem: I have a list of ten rules for behavior in my classroom, which I make sure are very clear. Sometimes the rules seem like a good idea, and sometimes they are a nuisance to enforce.

Whose Problem: The teacher's.

Analysis: A list of classroom rules imitates our American legal system, which carefully defines and enforces laws. Unfortunately, just as tax laws encourage taxpayers to search for loopholes, classroom rules defy students to misbehave in ways not written in the rules. Such behavior in the classroom can lead to confrontations between the student and the teacher. In addition, some rules may have exceptions requiring violation in unusual circumstances. For instance, a child may be required by his doctor to chew aspirin gum in class even though the class has a rule against gum chewing. This can also lead to confrontation from other students who also want to chew gum.

The best rules are those that cover all situations. They allow the teacher to correct, admonish or punish a misbehaving student whether he understood the rule or not. Such rules also encourage students to decide for themselves whether or not they are behaving correctly. If the students are a part of the system, they no longer try to beat it. They learn to act responsibly.

Do: 1) Establish only two rules in your classroom: a) The teacher and the students will treat everyone in the classroom with respect; and b) The teacher and the students will behave in a manner appropriate for the classroom. 2) If a student misbehaves, help him understand that he has acted inappropriately. If he is unable to do so, tell him when he is doing the wrong thing and explain why.

Do Not: 1) Do not waste time explaining the intricacies of a handful of rules. 2) Do not allow a student to get away with inappropriate behavior because he wasn't aware of a rule or his behavior wasn't covered by it.

Related Problems: 82 Controlling Class.

Problems with Procedures

♦ 133 ♦
Spanking

Problem: I was hired to teach in a private religious school where spanking of the smaller children is a part of school procedure. I'm not sure I want to spank children.

Whose Problem: The teacher's.

Analysis: Although almost every state has laws against physical punishment in the schools, the laws usually apply only to public schools. Many private and parochial institutions still allow and encourage spanking. This punishment may have a religious basis or be considered good old-fashioned discipline. Some parents and teachers support spanking and other forms of physical punishment because they work. They feel that children who are afraid of being paddled are less likely to act up in school than children who don't have to be afraid.

Most educators, however, are against physical punishment, because although it works, it has its price. It may encourage children to be violent. It may wrongfully demonstrate that might makes right. It may teach students that hitting is a way of resolving a problem or controlling a situation to get what you want. Consequently, many educators would rather use other types of punishment.

Do: 1) Decide if you can work in this environment. 2) If you are not comfortable with this procedure, seek work at another school.

Do Not: 1) Do not be the only person in the school who does not spank. 2) Do not spank children if you feel it is wrong. 3) Do not think you can reform the school.

Problems with Procedures

♦ 134 ♦
Students Invited to Teacher's Home

Problem: My class had a very good year. I am proud of the way the students worked. I would like to reward them. I thought of having a barbecue at my house, but another faculty member told me this was not proper.

Whose Problem: The teacher's.

Analysis: It is a good idea to reward students for a job well done, but the method must be appropriate. Teachers develop a comfortable teacher/student relationship with their classes. Inviting the students to a teacher's home crosses the boundaries of this relationship. The teacher may not have difficulty with this, but some of the students might feel uncomfortable. Many schools have restrictions on activities outside the school. In some school districts, accountability is as important as education. The barbecue may not be allowed anyway.

Do: 1) Find out the restrictions your school has for out-of-school activities after hours. 2) Decide if your activity obeys those restrictions. 3) If not, consider a trip during school hours or an activity inside the school, such as a party in your room, an after-school party in the school gym or pool, or a picnic on or near the school grounds. 4) Check with your administrator before proceeding.

Do Not: 1) Do not take students on activities away from the school without doing the necessary preparations and paperwork. 2) Do not bring students into your home.

Problems with Procedures

♦ 135 ♦
Substitute Teachers

Problem: I will be absent from school tomorrow. I hesitate to tell my class because they are so hard on substitute teachers.

Whose Problem: The students' or the teacher's.

Analysis: Students often act up when there is a substitute. They feel that when the teacher is gone the structure of the class is also gone. This indicates that the teacher is not preparing the class for a substitute. Sometimes this is an oversight, but other times the teacher is part of the problem because she has trouble sharing authority. She may be inadvertently teaching her class to behave only for her. She might feel good when she finds that the students did not behave well during her absence. She feels they are her children, and only she can control them.

Do: 1) If you are planning to be absent, tell your students there will be a substitute. 2) Tell them you expect the classroom procedures to continue without you and that you would like to feel proud of them for behaving well in your absence. 3) Leave notes about the classroom routines for the substitute. 4) Ask to be informed of any students who do not behave well. 5) When you return compliment those students who behaved well. Take appropriate measures with those who were reported as misbehaving. Students who learn to behave with a substitute will do so even during unplanned absences. 6) If you feel setting up this structure is difficult, you may have a problem sharing authority. Examine your feelings and your procedures regarding substitutes. Consider discussing the problem with a colleague.

Do Not: 1) Do not give mixed messages or unclear messages about your expectations during your absence. 2) Do not feel that if you are absent the day is lost for the class. 3) Do not feel that only you can control your group.

Problems with Procedures

◆ 136 ◆
Surprise Fire Drill

Problem: My class was in the gym wearing shorts and T-shirts when the fire alarm sounded. I had no way of knowing it was a routine drill. Although it was cold, I took them outside in their gym clothes because our hats and coats were in our room on another floor. I felt uncomfortable about this.

Whose Problem: The school administrator's.

Analysis: When the fire alarm sounds you must vacate the school, even if it seems like a bad idea. This is a fire regulation. When the fire alarm sounded there were three possibilities: it was a planned fire drill and the person in charge neglected to consider a class in the gym; the alarm sounded due to a malfunction or prank; or there was a fire and the building had to be evacuated.

Do: 1) Continue to take your class out of the school, regardless of the circumstances, when the fire alarm sounds. In a drill or a false alarm, a responsible person will see your class in their gym clothes and direct them back into the building. It will not harm them to be outside for a few minutes. If there is a fire, having no hats or coats will be a comparatively small problem. 2) Spend a few moments with your class considering what would have happened if the building really were on fire. 3) Ask your school planning committee or administration to consider better planning for fire drills.

Do Not: 1) Do not stay in the building. 2) Do not send anyone upstairs for hats and coats. 3) Do not delay leaving the building for any reason unless directly told by your administrator or the fire marshal.

Problems with Procedures

♦ 137 ♦
Teacher Dress Code

Problem: Our principal has instituted a dress code for the adults in the building. The men are required to wear slacks and ties. I am much more comfortable in jeans and gym shoes.

Whose Problem: The teacher's.

Analysis: Whether or not your principal has the right to establish standards of dress is determined by the school code and the teachers' contract. More importantly, a teacher's dress conveys a message to the students. School is a place of business—the business of learning. A teacher is a professional person engaged in that business and should dress accordingly. If a teacher is dressed as a professional, he is more likely to be treated with respect by both his students and the community.

Do: 1) Choose clothes which feel comfortable yet reflect the business side of you. You may notice that you feel more professional in front of your class dressed professionally. 2) Consider asking your class to dress up for a field trip. Note whether they behave differently when well dressed.

Do Not: 1) Do not think your choice of clothes is unimportant. 2) Do not fight with your principal over a dress code.

Related Problems: 138 Teachers Who Are Called by Their First Name.

Problems with Procedures

◆ 138 ◆
Teachers Who Are Called by Their First Name

Problem: I teach in a private school. Many of the teachers prefer to have the students call them by their first names and suggested that I do that too. I don't feel comfortable with this.

Whose Problem: The school procedure's.

Analysis: A teacher is a professional who deserves the respect of the students. Addressing the teacher in an appropriate manner demonstrates that respect. In contrast, some teachers allow students to call them by their first names because it helps create a relaxed, informal atmosphere. However, such an atmosphere also makes it easier for students to defy the teacher's authority and demonstrate a lack of respect.

Class structure is an essential element of the classroom. It is the foundation of all activities. Decorum is a part of that structure. Unless the class is highly motivated, proper decorum is a necessary component for learning.

Do: 1) Provide structure in your classroom. 2) Create an environment where it is not easy to question your decisions unless there is good cause to do so. Be somewhat formal with your students so they receive the message that you are a professional and your decisions are professional. 3) Insist your students call you by your last name with the proper title. 4) Suggest to your colleagues, especially those experiencing difficulties with classroom behavior, that they do the same with their students.

Do Not: 1) Do not create a relaxed, casual environment. 2) Do not allow students to call you by anything other than your correct last name. 3) Do not neglect to discuss this with colleagues who are having problems with their students.

Related Problems: 5 Calling Teacher by First Name, 137 Teacher Dress Code.

Problems with Procedures

◆ 139 ◆
Touching Students

Problem: A colleague of mine feels that in today's sensitive climate it is wise to avoid touching students. This seems cold to me, but, in light of the stories of students causing legal and personal problems with unwarranted accusations, I wonder if he is right.

Whose Problem: The teaching profession's.

Analysis: Accusations of sexual misconduct seem to occur frequently toward teachers in today's society. Some accusations result from improper touching. Others result from touching that is innocent, appropriate or non-existent.

No teacher wants to risk being brought in front of the principal or the courts accused of an impropriety. If the teacher is to be connected to the students however, some touching must take place. It is an important part of one human relating to another.

There are a number of ways to properly touch students. Shaking hands in the morning shows students the teacher is happy to see them and sometimes teaches the students how to shake hands. A "high five" rewards students for correct answers to tough problems. A pat on the shoulder can congratulate a successful student, and a touch on the arm can calm down an angry one.

Some teachers give hugs. These can be all right if done wisely. Hugs should be given side to side and not front to front. Smaller children should be given a pat on the head or a touch on the shoulder instead of a hug.

Do: 1) Be aware of children whose body language tells you they don't like to be hugged, or they like it too much. 2) Be conscious of the way a student reacts to your touch. 3) Realize that a good reputation as a teacher is a strong defense against such accusations.

Do Not: 1) Do not give hugs because you like them. 2) Do not make your students uncomfortable by touching them. 3) Do not have children sit on your lap. 4) Do not entirely avoid touching students. 5) Do not become fearful about touching your students or being accused of an impropriety. 6) Do not act unprofessionally.

Related Problems: 78 Accused by Student.

Chapter VIII

Problems with Unions

Union leaders are not the union. Union headquarter employees are not the union. You and the people who work alongside you in the schools are the union.

Problems with Unions

♦ 140 ♦
Dissatisfaction

Problem: Our school district has a union, but most of the teachers are dissatisfied with it. The union seldom manages to successfully negotiate our demands. We've never gone on strike.

Whose Problem: The teacher's or the union's.

Analysis: A union is made up of people who work in the same situation. They elect leaders every few years to represent them and protect them on their jobs. The role of union leaders is especially important during a pay dispute. In this situation teachers can never expect to get everything they request. The union should ask for more than they know will be given. The board will offer less than they know they will finally give. The two sides will work to a compromise.

Getting a raise is not a simple process. There are few ways to get the available funds, and all of them have problems. Raising taxes is unpopular and may cause taxpayers to move out of the area, thus lowering the tax base. Cutting programs means putting some teachers out of work and hurting the educational services for the children. A good union will put job security ahead of raises. A good union member will agree with this. In a good settlement, everyone walks away a little unhappy.

If a compromise cannot be reached, a strike is the last option. It is used when the union knows funds for a raise are available, but the board refuses to grant a raise. A strike should never be taken lightly. Strikes are disruptive and hurt all parties concerned. A union can be devastated by a strike that is lost. A good union leader will not take people out on strike unless there is a way to get them back in under any circumstance.

Do: 1) Invite your union leaders to meet with you and your faculty to discuss your concerns. 2) Ask them to explain their philosophies and policies in negotiating contracts. 3) Ask what other services they perform for the membership. 4) Evaluate your union leaders by answering the following questions:
    a) Do they maintain advantages already won in previous contracts?
    b) Are they responsive to the membership?
    c) Do they encourage the filing of grievances?

Problems with Unions

    d) Do they have a good record of winning grievances?
    e) Are they willing to work with government to improve working conditions?
    f) Are your raises keeping you ahead of inflation? Are they as good as can be expected considering the financial condition of your state and district?

5) If you answered no to any of these questions and know of someone else who could do the job better, vote the present leaders out of office.

Do Not: 1) Do not lose interest in working to keep your union strong. 2) Do not criticize your union unless you are certain that something is wrong. To do so would weaken both the union and yourself as a member.

Related Problems: 141 Going on Strike.

Problems with Unions

♦ 141 ♦
Going on Strike

Problem: Our union voted to go on strike. I voted against the strike because of the harm it will cause my students. I have heard many of them say that their teachers are abandoning them just for more money.

Whose Problem: The community's.

Analysis: Strikes usually occur when there is an impasse between the teachers and the board of education. Strikes should happen only as a last resort. They are difficult, unpopular, disruptive and must never be taken lightly. All parties involved—students, teachers, parents, and the community—lose something during a strike.

The teachers' union is the instrument through which the teachers deal with the board. It is organized democratically. Every member has a vote in important issues, but every member must also agree to abide by the decision of the majority. To do otherwise would be selfish and detrimental to the goals of the majority.

In a strike situation union leaders must have clearly-defined goals and a fallback plan for returning to work if it appears the strike cannot be won. Union members must remain unified. Members who decide to act contrary to the union plans give the board hope for winning the strike. Teachers who violate the wishes of the majority should expect a great deal of anger from their colleagues for having made an already difficult situation worse.

Do: 1) Before the strike begins, explain to your students that this strike must take place even if it is distasteful. Tell them that everyone hopes it will be short and not too disruptive. 2) If your students are old enough, consider explaining some of the details of the strike to them. 3) When the strike begins you should come to your school for picket duty. 4) If you find you are not in agreement with your union and feel you do not want to contribute to the strike effort, stay away from your school. Crossing a picket line generates resentment and ill feelings for a long time.

Problems with Unions

Do Not: 1) Do not feel that it is the teachers alone who are responsible for the strike. 2) Do not decide to work in spite of the strike. 3) Do not let the community believe that it is only the students who lose during a strike.

Related Problems: 140 Dissatisfaction.

Problems with Unions

♦ 142 ♦
No Representation

Problem: We have no union in our school district. I think we need one.

Whose Problem: The district teachers'.

Analysis: Most teachers realize the importance of being organized into a union when school administrators try to get as much as possible from their teachers while giving as little as possible. Unions provide their members with a collective strength which would not be possible were each member to act individually. Consequently it is not unusual for a teacher to feel union representation is necessary.

A teacher who initiates the idea of forming a union should expect resistance not only from administration, but from some faculty as well. Some teachers will oppose organizing because they feel it is unprofessional. Others will oppose it for philosophical reasons. Many of these are teachers who are earning the second wage in their family and are not solely dependent on their own wages and benefits. If successful, the union will provide a feeling of empowerment that should win over most of the faculty members who felt uneasy about joining.

Do: 1) Talk to your colleagues about the advantages of having a union for both representation and protection. 2) Determine the number of people in your school who want a union. 3) If 20% to 25% are in favor, you should proceed. For information specific to your situation contact:

> The American Federation of Teachers
> 555 New Jersey Avenue N.W.
> Washington, D.C. 20001
> 800-238-1133

> The National Education Association
> 1201 16th Street N.W.
> Washington, D.C. 20036
> 202-833-4000

Problems with Unions

Do Not: 1) Do not allow the situation to continue. 2) Do not let people tell you it is unprofessional to become unionized. 3) Do not fear a division in your work force over this issue. 4) Do not fear your district will fire you for union activities. (Be sure to specifically ask about this when you contact the unions.)

Problems with Unions

♦ 143 ♦
Poor Representation

Problem: The union representative in our school does not seem very responsive to us. She seems to go along with the principal more often than she does with the faculty.

Whose Problem: The faculty's.

Analysis: The school union representative plays a key role in the teachers' union as the link between union leadership and the members. The position is only as strong as the union representative makes it. With cooperation the job of union representative need not involve a lot of additional work. Fighting for and maintaining the rights of co-workers can provide occasions for appreciation and personal fulfillment. Union work is also an opportunity for growth and advancement within the union.

Unfortunately, the job of union representative is often viewed as one with many responsibilities and few rewards. It invites criticism from both administrators and faculty who feel they have been unfairly treated. Consequently, it is a position that can be difficult to fill. Principals may ask teachers loyal to them to run for the office so they can get and maintain control. If a union representative seems more loyal to the principal, this may be the case.

Do: 1) Recognize that your school representation reflects the involvement of the entire faculty. 2) Call your union headquarters and find out what is involved in being the school representative and how much of the duty can be shared by other faculty members. 3) Work with other faculty who care about union representation to find a willing candidate. 4) Make the position more attractive by adding rewards, such as a year-end luncheon. 5) Offer to relieve the candidate of some current duties so there is time to do the union work. 6) Give the candidate your collective support.

Do Not: 1) Do not allow poor representation to continue. 2) Do not blame the delegate you have for not doing enough.

Chapter IX

Suicide

- *All suicidal threats should be taken seriously.*
- *Many suicides can be prevented.*
- *If you find a student who is contemplating suicide, do all you can to get professional help for the student.*
- *If a student succeeds in committing suicide, the teacher should not feel responsible.*

Suicide

People commit suicide because they feel hopeless and despairing. They have been depressed for some time and feel that life is bad and isn't going to get better.

The current suicide rate for children under age 10 is almost nonexistent. For 10 to 14-year-olds it is one in 100,000 and increases tenfold for junior and senior high school students. The rise in teenage suicide in recent years is a source of major concern and may be worse than numbers indicate. It is important that educators correctly interpret the statistics discussed in many textbooks and college courses with the following points in mind:

    a) Drug overdoses, car crashes, and other causes of death are often classified as accidental although they may have been suicides. Therefore, the statistics are higher than reported.

    b) Suicides often occur in clusters. Teens who are close to each other may commit suicide together. Students who see the attention that suicide draws may commit "copy-cat" suicides. Therefore, while most schools have no suicides, others may have several.

    c) Though suicide rates show boys have a higher rate of suicide than girls, both boys and girls should be given equal attention.

    d) Though suicide rates show Caucasians have a higher suicide rate than other races, children of all races should be given equal attention.

Two statistics are most significant to the classroom teacher: a) the number of their students who have attempted suicide; and b) the number of their students who have succeeded in committing suicide. A teacher's aim is to have both these statistics be zero.

Unfortunately, not all student suicides can be prevented. A child who is determined to succeed at suicide will carry out a plan which is so secretive, nobody will suspect a thing. On the other hand, some students who are contemplating suicide become scared about what they are thinking. Often they will find a way for a person they trust, such as a teacher, to discover their plan in time to stop them.

Many textbooks alert readers of suicidal warning signs. The list of signs usually include

    a) sudden changes in behavior,
    b) serious academic or social problems,
    c) substance abuse,
    d) problems at home,
    e) breakup of a romantic relationship or close friendship,

Suicide

f) separation or divorce of parents, and
g) disturbed peer relationships.

However, junior high and high school teachers will find that many of their students experience these problems during the school year with no threat of potential suicide. To watch every student with these problems for potential suicide would be time consuming and would probably not be helpful.

Many texts recommend that when a student indicates suicidal feelings the teacher take all suicidal threats seriously, establish communication with the student, and provide emotional support. Though this is good advice, each recommendation has its own problems. If a student talks about suicide, can the teacher determine whether the student is joking or serious and confront the student effectively? How should the teacher respond if the student was just joking? What does a teacher say to a student who has just confided a plan to commit suicide? How much emotional support should a teacher provide to a suicidal student and in what form?

Effective suicide prevention cannot be a plan which is put into effect at a time of crisis. It must be a part of the classroom culture. The teacher must establish an atmosphere in which everyone understands they are part of a group that is functioning together—they need everyone and everyone needs them. They have a purpose. What they do affects the others.

If a student is depressed, people around the student care. The teacher must show this with actions and words—acknowledge the student's depression and problems; express hope that the student will feel better soon; and offer encouragement and support until the student gets through the depression.

A teacher must recognize that a student who mentions or discusses suicide or killing in conversation, personal notes, or writing assignments is engaging in suicidal behavior. This is cause for alarm. The student must be confronted. The school administration and the student's family must be notified.

Although teachers should be prepared to assist in helping a suicidal student, they must recognize that suicidal behavior is a problem beyond their expertise. Teachers should know the resources available, such as a school counselor, a local community outreach program, a suicide hot line or a crisis prevention drop-in center, and seek such help immediately when a student is reaching despair. If a student confides a plan to commit suicide to a teacher, it can be the beginning of the problem's resolution.

Suicide

♦ 144 ♦
Threatened

Problem: One of my students told me that if I fail him on next week's exam, he will kill himself. I don't think he is serious, but it scares me. I may have to exempt him from taking the exam.

Whose Problem: The student's.

Analysis: This student may be serious about killing himself, but, because of the way he approached the teacher, there is a strong chance he is not. However, he is being manipulative and uncaring by making such a statement. It is his responsibility to pass the test, not the teacher's. Threatening the teacher may be his way of passing on the responsibility when he should be studying for the test instead. It may never be known how serious the student was about the threat. However, if it does seem the student is serious, the teacher must ignore the test and seek help for the student.

Do: 1) Tell the student you are concerned about what he told you. 2) Acknowledge that he may be feeling desperate about the exam. Try to get him to discuss his situation with you and work out a better way to cope with this test. Offer suggestions for helping him study. 3) Discuss the way he approached you, and inform him that you found it threatening and irresponsible. 4) Tell him that you will have to report his threat to the administration, even if he didn't mean it. If the student is unwilling to discuss this with you, you still must report the incident to your administrator or counselor. 5) If he insists he was joking, report that as well. 6) If necessary, excuse the student from the test until a resolution is reached.

Do Not: 1) Do not panic or get upset. 2) Do not feel his life is in your hands. 3) Do not try to help him out of his predicament. This is the work of a professional trained in this area. 4) Do not neglect to report the incident to your administrator. 5) Do not allow the student to manipulate you.

Related Problems: 145 Potential.

Suicide

◆ 145 ◆
Potential

Problem: A student in one of my classes came to me today and told me he is thinking of killing himself.

Whose Problem: The student's.

Analysis: The student may be in such despair that he is seriously thinking of killing himself, or he may be desperately seeking attention. It is not necessary to decide his intention. Either is a serious matter that requires the same response. If the boy is contemplating suicide, his action demonstrates that he is searching for a way out. He has come to you to provide a way out for him. If he had already decided on suicide as his only option, he would not tell anyone. They might try to stop him. It is important that, regardless of the teacher's discomfort, the boy's comment should be taken seriously.

If the teacher feels the student just needs attention, it is important to give him attention. To consider it a bluff and brush him off would be a mistake. Potential suicides who feel they are not being taken seriously may carry out their suicide to show they were not kidding.

Do: 1) Acknowledge the seriousness of what he has told you. 2) Give him an opportunity to talk, keeping in mind that his problems may seem solvable to you but are overwhelming to him. 3) Without trying to resolve his problems, acknowledge their seriousness. 4) Underscore that suicide need not be the solution. Other solutions are reachable. You would like to see him find them.

Here is a dramatization of what the responses might be. This is only one example. You may feel more effective or more comfortable with another approach.

Student: Mrs. Jones, I am seriously thinking of killing myself.
Teacher: John, my goodness. What are you saying? This sounds very serious. Tell me what is going on.

Student: Everything is so hopeless.
Teacher: Yes, it certainly sounds like you are having a very rough time of it now, but I am really concerned about your plans to kill yourself. I would feel very sad if that

Suicide

were to happen. I certainly hope you are not going to carry this out. [He may have been hoping someone with some control would tell him not to do it]. It seems to me you have some other options. Problems can be worked out without going to this extreme. I think we can look for some options together.

Student: What do you mean?
Teacher: You and I should share what you have told me with Mr. Smith.

Student: The counselor? I don't know if I want to go see him.
Teacher: I'll go with you. If you are not comfortable with him, I'm sure he can suggest someone else.

5) Suggest that you go together to speak to the school counselor, psychologist or social worker because they are better trained in this area than you. 6) Do everything you can to get him to talk with a professional counselor while he is still with you. Do not send him. Take him. 7) Tell the counselor what the boy has told you. 8) End your participation at this point, other than periodically asking the boy how he is doing. 9) If you are unable to get him to see a counselor, report the incident to your school administration immediately. In most states this is the law. 10) Report the incident to his parents, or ask the counselor or administrator to do so. Tell the boy you are going to do this because you are required by law and because you are concerned about him. 11) Regardless of how it sounds, make him promise not to do anything drastic or violent to himself.

Do Not: 1) Do not assume the student just wants attention. 2) Do not feel overwhelmed. 3) Do not try to minimize the problem. 4) Do not try to handle the problem by yourself. 5) Do not neglect to notify a member of your counseling staff, administration and the parents. 6) Do not report the incident without telling the boy. He may feel betrayed.

Related Problems: 86 Helping a Student with Personal Problems, 146 Student Reports Friend.

Suicide

◆ 146 ◆
Student Reports Friend

Problem: A student in my class just told me that her friend is talking about killing herself.

Whose Problem: The friend's or the student's.

Analysis: The student reporting her friend may actually be the one with suicidal thoughts, or the friend may be hoping the student will stop her from committing suicide. Either way the student talking to you is overwhelmed and asking for help.

Do: 1) Inquire who the friend is. 2) Whether she tells you or not, ask if she can bring the friend in to talk to you. She need not tell her friend what it is about. If she seems to vacillate or hesitate, she may be talking about herself. 3) Try to establish what she wants to discuss. 4) If she backs off, report this to a school counselor and an administrator. Proceed in the same manner suggested in problem 145. 5) If she seems willing to bring in her friend, then most likely she is not the one to be concerned about. 6) Ensure that they both return by the next day. 7) When the students return, speak to them together. 8) Make the suicidal girl feel as comfortable as you can. Do not let her feel betrayed by her friend. Tell her she is lucky to have a friend who cares so much about her. 9) Mention you have heard she has been saying some scary things, such as talking seriously about death. You would like to hear some of the things she has been saying. 10) If she admits to contemplating suicide, proceed as in problem 145, points 1-8. 11) If she does not respond openly, proceed as in problem 145, points 9-10. 12) If you cannot get her involved with another adult in the building, contact her parents immediately and try to stay with her until her parents come to school to get her.

Do Not: 1) Do not dismiss the problem because you didn't get enough information. 2) Do not dismiss the problem because one or both girls would not cooperate. 3) Do not fail to report this to the school counselor and administrator. 4) Do not try to solve the girl's problems.

Related Problems: 86 Helping a Student with Personal Problems, 145 Potential.

Suicide

♦ 147 ♦
Completed

Problem: A boy in my homeroom committed suicide over the weekend. I can't help wondering if I could have said or done something that would have stopped him.

Whose Problem: The teacher's and many of the boy's friends'.

Analysis: The tragic occurrence of a student suicide will cause at various times feelings of loss, frustration, anger, and guilt among teachers and students. Shock turns to grief, grief is followed by anger, and anger causes frustration and guilt. All of these feelings are natural.

Suicide is seldom caused by a single event, but rather by a buildup of many. Those who are intent on committing suicide do not want to be stopped and, therefore, do not give signals. In retrospect a teacher may think that clues of suicidal tendencies were missed, but similar behavior could have been observed in many non-suicidal students. This student had many problems of which the teacher was unaware and could not have solved anyway. The teacher is not at fault. The teacher is, however, faced with another challenge—to provide the strength and guidance to hold the class together while everyone, teacher and students, cope with personal feelings.

Many students in the class will be confused about the events and unsure of their feelings. They will look to the teacher for comfort and guidance. Teachers who express feelings, even through tears, teach the students normal, healthy responses and demonstrate that they care about their students and would grieve for them too.

Unfortunately, there may also be students who will be enticed by the attention the suicide brings and consider the option themselves. They too may remain silent in their thoughts, creating the danger that copycat suicides may occur. Many schools provide professional counselors to prevent such outbreaks and to help both students and teachers cope with the initial tragedy.

Do: 1) Accept that you could not have prevented your student's suicide. 2) If professional grief counselors come to your homeroom, offer to stay—though they understand grief, you understand your students. The session may also help you. 3) Be pre-

Suicide

pared to answer your students' questions. Demonstrate that you care for them. Let them talk freely. 4) Talk about the negative aspects of the boy's suicide. Mention that many people who knew the victim, including his classmates, may be feeling angry at him and that it is all right to feel that way. Stress that although many people are thinking about the boy now, as time passes, he will become more and more forgotten. If someone decides to stop living, the rest of the world goes on without him. 5) Cry if you feel the need and are comfortable doing so. However, if you feel you may lose control of yourself ask a colleague to cover your class for you until you are better composed. 6) If any of your students question the value of committing suicide, make it very clear that they may not commit suicide. 7) Consider asking them to promise they will never commit suicide and cause the class to feel sad again.

Do Not: 1) Do not feel that you had some role in causing the suicide. 2) Do not feel you can always detect a potential suicide. 3) Do not feel you should hide your emotions from your class. However, do not allow yourself to completely fall apart. 4) Do not feel that professional grief counselors can be more comforting to your students than you can.

Related Problems: Introduction to this section, 86 Helping a Student with Personal Problems.

Chapter X

Fighting

Teaching is not meant to be a high-risk occupation.

Fighting

Years ago when students were caught fighting they would run away or stop fighting when the teacher arrived. An anxious audience would part as the teacher moved in to separate the two fighters, who would then be brought to the principal's office to receive their punishments.

This scenario has become rare in today's society. The influence of mass media, pressure of gang affiliation, and availability of weapons have made fighting in schools more prevalent and dangerous. Students bring knives, razors, or guns to school. Crowds prevent teachers from approaching the scene. Fighters seldom stop when teachers arrive. Teachers may be shoved aside, pushed down, or injured by weapons.

In the past, teachers have always felt that breaking up fights was part of their school duty. However, this may no longer be wise, unless it can be accomplished without getting hurt. The teacher witnessing the fight must make this decision. The principal, whose job is to see that the school runs smoothly, may not agree with the decision. However, it is better for the teacher to be reprimanded in the principal's office than to be congratulated in the emergency room.

Fighting

♦ 148 ♦
Small Children

Problem: There are two boys in my third grade class who are always fighting with each other. I must separate them several times a day. Although they are friends again after each fight, I am concerned that one of them will cause an injury to the other.

Whose Problem: The two boys'.

Analysis: The boys could be fighting for many reasons: they are disbursing pent-up energy; they are filling a need for physical contact, which they get from each other and from the teacher when they are restrained; or they need periodic breaks in their routine. Whatever their reasons, the boys complement one another. That is why they found each other and maintain their friendship. Each enables the other to get something he needs. However, their fighting is unacceptable. They must be taught to behave appropriately.

Do: 1) Tell the boys together that this fight is finished. Fighting will no longer be tolerated in class or on school grounds. 2) Institute a consequence for breaking this rule, such as removal from the class for a period of time after each incident. 3) Seat the boys on opposite sides of the room. 4) If they start fighting again, which is a strong possibility, stand over them and count to five. If they haven't separated by then, increase their consequence. 5) Ask another teacher for future assistance if one of the boys must be briefly removed from your room. 6) Discuss your plan with the principal in case you should need back up. 7) Notify the parents of the boys' behavior and your new procedure to rectify the situation. 8) Set up a reward for days they have no incidents. 9) Give the boys classroom duties which will allow them to appropriately move about the room to expend some of their energy.

Do Not: 1) Do not allow the situation to continue. 2) Do not get physically involved with separating the students. 3) Do not brush it off as only boys' play.

Related Problems: 25 Hitting Another Student, 27 Hitting the Teacher, 31 Insulting Another Student, 139 Touching Students.

Fighting

♦ 149 ♦
Older Boys

Problem: There is a lot of tension at our high school due to two rival gangs. Our principal said he expects the teachers to break up fights in our rooms and in the halls. Some of these boys are pretty big, and I am afraid of getting injured.

Whose Problem: The students' and the principal's.

Analysis: The unfortunate increase in drugs, weapons and gangs in our society has caused an increase in violence in our schools. Though the American public has voiced concern for the safety of students, there should also be concern for the safety of the teachers.

When a fight occurs, teachers have two responsibilities—to try to keep everyone safe and to try to restore order. Many people think it is also the duty of a teacher to break up fights. Some principals demand it from their faculty. However, many teachers are injured disrupting these fights. Though teachers are responsible for safety in the classroom, that safety must include their own and that of innocent students. It must take priority over the well-being of those students who have chosen to fight.

A teacher can consider breaking up a fight only if
 a) eye contact can be made with one of the fighters,
 b) either fighter responds to his name,
 c) either fighter looks like he doesn't want to fight, or
 d) the teacher feels the situation can be handled without getting hurt.

A teacher should stay away from the fight if
 a) either fighter has a weapon,
 b) the fighters have locked eyes and are ignoring the teacher,
 c) either fighter looks out of control, or
 d) the teacher is afraid of getting hurt.

Do: 1) Get help at the first sign of an approaching fight by calling the office or sending a student to get help from a nearby adult. 2) If this does not cause the tension to subside, tell the students who want to fight to sit on opposite sides of the room immediately. 3) If they will not separate, order the other students to move out of the way and be quiet. This will ensure their safety and prevent them from encouraging the fighters—some students

Fighting

may find fights entertaining or have a particular interest in one of the fighters. 4) If any of the other students do not obey you, call them by name so they know you are aware of the role they are playing.

If a fight ensues and you decide to intervene: 1) Approach the boy you feel is less threatening. Continue eye contact with him while gently pushing him back and softly tell him to calm down. 2) Quickly turn to the other boy, call him by name and tell him to back off. 3) Stay in between them and let everyone catch their breath. 4) If they start to fight again and push you out of the way, or try to fight around you, or totally ignore you, move out of the way. 5) If you manage to restore peace, have the two fighters sit apart from each other. 6) Appear appropriately angry and yell at them a little. When another adult arrives, send both fighters out of the room with him.

If you decide not to intervene: 1) Keep an eye on the fight from a safe distance until help arrives. 2) When another adult arrives, send both fighters out of the room with him. 3) Explain to your principal that the situation was too threatening for you to intervene. 4) Give consequences to the students who encouraged the two boys to fight or prevented you from intervening. 5) Remind the class that your room is a safe place and those who violate the safety will be punished. 6) If your school does not have a policy about fighting which takes the teachers' safety into consideration, work with other faculty members to adopt one.

Do Not: 1) Do not feel you must break up the fight. 2) Do not panic. 3) Do not neglect to send for help. 4) Do not stand by helplessly. 5) Do not get hurt. 6) Do not feel guilty if you don't feel it is safe for you to intervene. 7) Do not let your principal reprimand you for seeking to avoid personal injury.

Related Problems: 25 Hitting Another Student, 27 Hitting the Teacher, 150 Older Girls.

Fighting

♦ 150 ♦
Older Girls

Problem: Two girls in our high school got into a violent fight. I was going to break it up, but it didn't seem safe.

Whose Problem: The girls'.

Analysis: Because women are less prone to fight physically than men, our culture portrays many examples of men fighting and few of women. Men learn to fight from these many examples, but women, do not. Therefore, girls are less predictable than boys when fighting. They know they want to hurt the other person but may not be sure how to go about it. They may slap, punch, bite, scratch or pull hair. When it seems the fight is over there is a chance it will start up again.

Do: 1) Determine whether to intervene using the method stated in problem 149. 2) Consider that fighting girls may be less predictable than fighting boys.

Do Not: 1) Do not intervene if you don't feel safe. 2) Do not fail to send for help as soon as the fight starts. 3) Do not feel it is solely your responsibility to stop the fight. 4) Do not let other students get involved with the fight.

Related Problems: 25 Hitting Another Student, 27 Hitting the Teacher, 149 Older Boys.

Index

Abuse: physical, 48; sexual, 57; suspected, 64; threatened, 70
Accused, by student, 88
Acting out, 2
Administrative support, lack of, 127, 129
Advancing in career, 90
Advice: giving, 98; sought, 138
Anger, 91
Apologizing, 3
Assignments, additional; 122, 123
Attention: getting, 3; lack of, 40; maintaining, 147
Attraction: to student, 95; to teacher, 14

Black English, 27
Boredom, 92
Borrowing: money, 5; supplies, 54

Calls teacher by first name, 6
Chasing, 7
Cheating, 8
Chewing gum, 9
Changing grades, 125
Cigarettes, 61
Class clown, 10
Class goat, 11
Class load, over maximum, 148
Classical literature, 146
Clinging parent, 137, 139
Clothing, provocative, 52
Clout: exerted, 132; threatened, 133
Control, of class, 93
Cooperation, lack of: from aid, 119; from colleague, 120; from parent, 141, 142; from principal, 127, 129
Correcting, the teacher, 13
Counseling, 98
Crush: on student, 95; on teacher, 14
Cults, 15
Curtailed program, 124
Cursing, 65

Death, of student, 21
Depressed: teacher, 97, 106; student, 17, 78

Discipline, 79
Discrimination: toward students, 96; faculty 110, 112
Disinterested parent, 142
Dislikes child, 135
Divorce, 19
Dress code, 156
Drugs: colleague using, 118; lecture, 20; selling, 56; usage, 59
Dying, student, 21

Ebonics, 27
Epilepsy, 23
Ethnic superiority, 96
Extra duties, 122, 123

Failing school work, 49
Father's Day presents, 24
Fighting: small children, 179; older boys, 180; older girls, 182
Fire drill, 155
First name, calling teacher by, 6, 157
Foreign student, 25

Gangs, 26
Ghetto English, 27
Gifted student, 28; parent believes, 134
Goat, of the class, 11
Going on strike, 162
Grades, 80; changes, 125; physical education, 149
Gum chewing, 9

Harassment, 126
Hate: job, 97; teacher, 30
Helping student with problems, 98
Hitting: culturally accepted, 32; student, 31; teacher 33
Home phone number, 99
Holiday party, 112
Homeless, 34
Homework, 35

Impulsive student, 36
Inattention, 40
Inclusion, 81
Inner-city teaching, 146
Insulting: student, 37; teacher, 38

Index

Juvenile delinquent, 39
Learning disabilities, 83
Leaving class, student, 41
Liked, wanting to be, 107
Low I.Q., 58, 85
Lying, 43

Mainstreaming, 81
Marijuana, 59
Motivation, 44

Notes from parents, 136

Obscene computer message, 45
Off-task, 46
Older teacher, 114
Out-of-control student, 74
Over-protective parent, 137, 139
Over maximum class load, 148

Parent, clinging, 137, 139
Parental note inappropriate, 136
Parents: divorcing, 19; yelling, 143
Parties: for faculty, 112; special education, 84; students, 153
Passive student, 47
Personal advice: giving, 98; sought, 138
Personal attention, 4
Personal: crisis, 100; politics, 101; values, 102
Phone number, teacher's home, 99
Physical abuse, 48
Physical education grades, 149
Poor teaching, 113
Poor school work, 49, 108
Power struggles, 50
Praise, 103
Pregnant student, 51; secretive, 55
Prejudice: against students, 96; against teachers, 110, 112
Program cuts, 150
Provocative clothing, 52
Punishment, 104, 152

Recreational reading, 53
Representation by union, 164, 166
Retarded student, 58, 85, 103
Rewards, 153
Rules, 151

Selling drugs, 56
Sexual abuse, 57
Sexual advance: from colleague, 116; from principal, 128
Sleep, losing, 106
Slow student, 58, 85, 103
Smell: dirty, 60; of marijuana, 59; of tobacco, 61
Smoking: cigarettes, 61; marijuana, 59
Spanking, 152
Stealing: by colleague, 117; from class, 62; from community, 63
Strikes, 162
Student teacher, poor, 115
Substance abuse: by colleague, 118; by student, 56, 59
Substitutes, 154
Successful teaching, 105
Suicidal threats, 170, 171, 173
Suicide, 174
Supplies, 54
Suspected abuse, 64
Swearing, 65

Talking excessively, 66
Tantrums, 67
Tardiness, 68
Tattletale, 69
Text book selection, 140
Theft, 62, 63, 117
Threatening the teacher, 71
Threatening suicide, 170, 171, 173
Thrown out of home, 34
Touching of students, 158; of teacher 72
Truancy, 73

Uncontrollable student, 74
Uncooperative: aid, 119; colleague, 120; parent, 141, 142; principal, 127, 129
Unions, 160, 162, 164, 166

Walking out, student, 41
Wheel chair, 78, 86
Whining, 75
Withdrawn student, 76
Worried about the class, 108

Yelling parent, 143